Amazing Facts in Canadian History

Grades 4-6

Written by Frances Stanford
Illustrated by Ric Ward

ISBN 1-55035-731-X
Copyright 2003
Revised April 2007
All Rights Reserved * Printed in Canada

Published in Canada by:
S&S Learning Materials
15 Dairy Avenue
Napanee, Ontario
K7R 1M4
www.sslearning.com

Look For

OTHER CANADIAN UNITS

AMAZING FACTS IN CANADIAN HISTORY

Table of Contents

AMAZING FACTS IN CANADIAN HISTORY

Introduction

Those who study Canadian history are presented with two problems. The first problem is that some interesting or enjoyable stories are ignored because those who write the history books do not consider them to be important. Some examples are:

> Pierre Elliott Trudeau and Jean Chretien do not use their first names.
> Louis Riel thought he was a prophet.
> Sir John Abbott, who later became Prime Minister, was a good friend of Hugh Allen who tried to bribe the federal government.
> Sir John A. Macdonald had to walk to visit his clients because he could not afford to buy a horse and buggy.
> Arthur Meighen could recite Shakespeare.

The second problem is that sometimes the facts that are presented as history cannot be truly documented. For example:

> It was widely recognized that Robert E. Peary was the first white man to see the North Pole. However, many historians claim that this is not true.
> There may or may not be a monster called Ogopogo in Lake Okanagan in British Columbia.
> Did St. Brendan actually discover North America before the Vikings while searching for Brazil?

Pre-learning Activities

This book is designed as a series of quizzes that includes many strange and amazing facts of Canadian history. It does not deal with all of the important facts that students learn in school. Instead, by revealing little known facts, it gives a personal, intimate view of the people and events that made Canada what it is today. Each section of this book is designed to be used as a pre-learning activity. Prior to studying an event or a period in Canadian history, one of these quizzes could be used to arouse the students' interest or curiosity and help them to attain a different perspective on what they are about to learn. It should be used as a starting point for discussion.

The answers and the facts to support them are included after each quiz. The details needed to elaborate on the answer enables the student to further understand these historical events. There are also puzzles and logic problems included in this book. There are historical mysteries which ask the students to become historical detectives. The teacher can assign these mysteries to groups of students to solve or can present the mystery to the class and play a game of "Twenty Questions" to help the students figure out the answer. If the twenty questions routine is followed, the teacher should instruct the students on how to ask questions that require a "Yes" or "No" answer, but at the same time giving them the information they need.

The students can also start their own list of strange and unusual facts that they come across in their research throughout the year. They can also illustrate strange and unusual events on a bulletin board devoted to this subject.

Native Peoples

The native peoples of Canada were the first inhabitants of the land now known as Canada. They often refer to themselves as **First Nations**. They lived together in many different tribes, that each had its own customs, language and religion, in every natural region of the country. The native peoples of Canada spoke 53 different languages. They hunted in the forests and on the plains, and fished in the oceans, rivers and streams. The frozen North was home to the Eskimo and Inuit who survived on the tundra. These were the first Canadians who welcomed the Europeans and traded with them. The native peoples adopted the European language, clothing and customs and taught them how to survive in this new land. Later, the Europeans tried to adapt the natives to farming and wage labour. This opened up new opportunities for the natives but it also cost them their traditional way of life.

Here are some strange and little known facts about the First Nations of Canada and their lives before the coming of the Europeans. Since there were so many diverse tribes, some of these facts may only apply to one or a few, and not to all.

1. The Plateau people sometimes spent the winter in **pit houses** which were often:
   a) on the seashore.   **b)** on the ice.   **c)** in the forest.   **d)** partly underground.

2. The Inuit hunters used a _____ when they were hunting seals.
   a) kayak   **b)** spear   **c)** feather   **d)** net

3. Which of the following did the Inuit use in the spring?
   a) snow goggles   **b)** umiaks   **c)** ear plugs   **d)** dog teams

4. A game invented by the Inuit was:
   a) checkers.   **b)** cat's cradle   **c)** basketball   **d)** baseball

5. The natives that farmed used a method of farming called:
   a) terracing.   **b)** irrigation.   **c)** slash and burn. **d)** crop rotation.

6. The Micmac people grew:
   a) tobacco.   **b)** potatoes.   **c)** rice.   **d)** lettuce.

7. Who did the natives believe was responsible for all living things in their present form?
   a) the Great Spirit   **b)** the sun   **c)** a trickster   **d)** the moon

8. The medicine man of the tribe was called a:
   a) chief.   **b)** shaman.   **c)** warrior.   **d)** meat eater.

9. The skins were processed mainly by the:
    a) children.   **b)** slaves.   **c)** women.   **d)** men.

10. Girls were required to seclude themselves from the boys when they reached:
    a) fifteen.   **b)** puberty.   **c)** five.   **d)** old age.

11. Men became members of different societies by:
    a) marrying into that society.   **b)** becoming a great hunter.
    c) becoming a great warrior.   **d)** purchasing a bundle from that society.

12. The natives who hunted buffalo used the bladder of the buffalo as a:
    a) water bag.   **b)** football.   **c)** pot.   **d)** mocassin.

13. The main food for the Northwest People was the:
    a) salmon.   **b)** whale.   **c)** beaver.   **d)** muskrat.

14. A cannibal monster the natives threatened their children with was called the:
    a) Bogeyman.   **b)** Piranha.   **c)** Windigo.   **d)** Loch Ness.

15. The clothes were sometimes decorated with:
    a) whalebones.   **b)** porcupine quills.   **c)** leaves.   **d)** flowers.

Answer Key

1. **d) partly underground**. In the winter, the Plateau people lived in pit houses dug into the ground - often in the bank of a creek. The walls were built of logs and sealed with earth and bark. The dome shaped roof was covered with boughs and poles and was insulated with earth and grass.

2. **c) feather** - The hunters would gather at a seal breathing hole in the ice. They would put a feather on the water in the hole. When the feather moved, they knew that a seal was breathing on it, and then they would use a harpoon to kill the seal.

3. **a) snow goggles**. They used snow goggles made from pieces of ivory or wood with long, narrow openings for the eyes to prevent snow blindness.

4. **b) cat's cradle**

5. **c) slash and burn**. The men cleared the land with stone axes and then burned it.

6. **a) tobacco**. The Micmac were the only natives to grow tobacco.

7. **c) a trickster** which was different in each tribe.

8. **b) shaman**.

9. **c) women**.

10. **b) puberty**. They also had to wear a large puberty hood during that period which might last over a year.

11. **d) purchasing a bundle from that society**. The medicine bundles were the focus of religious societies. Men purchased bundles from a junior society from its owners, who in turn purchased a bundle from another society.

12. **a) water bag**.

13. **a) salmon**.

14. **c) Windigo**. The windigo was a cannibal monster who killed humans to satisfy his enormous appetite.

15. **b) porcupine quills**. These were usually dyed different colours.

Name: _____

Pictographs

Evidence that the early native groups of Canada used symbols for writing has been found in caves and on the rocks along the shoreline of many rivers.

Can you interpret these symbols?

1.

_____

6.

_____

11.

_____

16.

_____

2.

_____

7.

_____

12.

_____

17.

_____

3.

_____

8.

_____

13.

_____

18.

_____

4.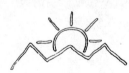

_____

9.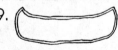

_____

14.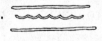

_____

19.

_____

5.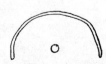

_____

10.

_____

15.

_____

20.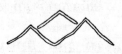

_____

Name: _____

Native Legend

Here is a legend about how one of the main groups of native peoples became farmers. Read the legend and follow the directions below to find out the name of that group.

Once, a great hunter was on a journey. After a long day, he went to sleep by his fire. Suddenly he woke. A woman was standing near the fire. "The Great Spirit has sent me to marry you," she said.

The hunter had never seen the woman before, but he agreed right away. "We will do as the Great Spirit wishes," he said.

The hunter spent a happy winter with his new wife. In the spring he took her back to his people.

Now, the hunter's people had always found their food by hunting and fishing. They did not know anything about growing food.

The Great Spirit had given corn seeds to the hunter's wife. She gave them to the people. "Let us dig beds in the earth for the seeds to lie in," she told them. "Let us cover the seeds softly and watch over them. By and by, they will come to life."

Sure enough, that is what happened. Tiny green plants began to grow in the sunshine. They looked like a strange kind of grass. As the plants grew, they formed long green 'ears'. Inside these ears grew plump yellow cobs of corn.

Answer the following questions on the spaces provided. Use the letters in the circles to form the words which will tell you the name of this group of native peoples.

1. They used the _ O O _ _ _ to make mats and O _ _ _ _ _ _ _ _.

2. The dry corn _ O _ _ _ _ _ were used to make dolls.

3. The women made _ O _ _ _ _ _ _ _ _ _ from the kernels.

4. _ _ O O O _ _ _ _ were cooked in the fire.

5. Dried _ O O _   _ _ _ O _ _ _ were used to make rattles.

— — — — — — —

— — — —

PLANTERS

Name: _____

The Vikings

The first Europeans to visit the shores of North America were Norse farmers and traders from Greenland called Vikings. According to their sagas, they discovered the coast of North America when their ships were blown off course on voyages between Greenland and Europe.

The Vikings were people from Norway, Denmark and Sweden who traded with those who could defend themselves and raided and pillaged those who could not.

Bjarni Herjolfsson was the first Viking to see the land of North America in 986, but he refused to land. He returned to Greenland with his stories of the new land. About fifteen years later, Leif Ericsson sailed the course taken by Bjarni and settled in Vinland (now believed to be Newfoundland) for the winter. He returned with tales of abundant salmon, timber and grapes. A few years later, about 1010, Thorfinn Karlsefini returned to Vinland with settlers and traders and established a settlement. His son, Snorri, was the first European to be born in the New World. After fighting with the natives, he decided to leave the settlement three years later. Archaeologists have found the remains of a Viking settlement at L'Anse aux Meadows, Newfoundland.

See if you are able to discover some little known facts about the Vikings. Read each of the following sentences and circle the letter of the correct answer.

1. The word Viking means:
   a) traveller   **b)** pirate
   c) trader   **d)** farmer

2. The Vikings did not have a (an):
   a) compass.   **b)** language.
   c) army.   **d)** navy.

3. One of the great archaeological discoveries at L'Anse aux Meadows was a:
   a) wrench.   **b)** spear.
   c) a spindle whorl.   **d)** maps.

4. The Viking clothing was mainly made of:
   a) furs.   **b)** wool.
   c) leaves.   **d)** skin.

5. Saturday was the day on which the Vikings:
   a) went dancing.   **b)** went to church.
   c) went fishing.   **d)** had a bath.

6. The most important animal to the Vikings was the:
   a) horse.   **b)** dog.
   c) sheep.   **d)** pig.

7. _____ was a very important sport to the Vikings:
   a) Swimming   **b)** Archery
   c) Running   **d)** Rowing

8. Instead of writing on paper, the Vikings used:
   a) leaves.   **b)** bark.
   c) stone.   **d)** glass.

9. The average Viking wore a jacket made of:
   a) leather.   **b)** wool.
   c) fur.   **d)** linen.

10. The _____ was the most valued Viking weapon:
    a) spear   **b)** rifle
    c) knife   **d)** sword

11. The Vikings were the only fighters in Europe to use a (an):
    a) word.   **b)** axe.
    c) spear.   **d)** rifle.

12. Viking children were considered to be adults at:
    a) 15 years of age.   **b)** 20 years of age.
    b) 12 years of age.   **d)** 10 years of age.

13. The games played by the Vikings were very similar to:
    a) chess.   **b)** monopoly.
    c) poker.   **d)** crossword puzzles.

14. The _____ was the most expensive part of a Viking ship:
    a) mast   **b)** galley
    c) sail   **d)** prow

15. _____ was the most powerful Viking god:
    a) Thor   **g)** Odin
    c) Frigg   **d)** Mjoollnir

Answer Key

1. **a) pirate**

2. **c) compass.** They sailed by using their knowledge of the sun, moon and stars.

3. **c) a spindle whorl.** It is 1.25 inches in width and carved from soapstone. It is used as a fly wheel on a wool spinning machine.

4. **b) wool.** They raised sheep and the women spun the wool to make clothes. Linen was also used.

5. **d) had a bath.** Viking farms had a sauna or a bath house nearby for their weekly baths.

6. **d) pig** - was the most important animal to the Vikings.

7. **b) archery** - All Vikings had to be able to shoot a bow and arrow.

8. **c) stone.** The Vikings chiseled their words into stone. These markings have been called runes.

9. **a) leather.**

10. **d) sword** - The Vikings believed one's sword brought good luck and protection in battle.

11. **b) axe.** It was called a battle-axe and could be of two types: one that was thrown or one that was wielded by the warrior.

12. **d) 10 years of age.** They were expected to work at the age of five.

13. **a) chess**

14. **c) sails.** The sails were made from wool or linen and often cost more than the rest of the ship. They were often trimmed with leather and were made in small triangular pieces

15. **b) Odin**

A Mystery From History

The Beothucks

When the Vikings arrived in the New World, they traded and fought with natives that lived in the area. They called these natives **Skraelings** and from the description of them, they were the same tribe of natives encountered by the first English settlers to Newfoundland. The name which has been given to this group of native people is **Beothuck**. However, the name given to them by the first Europeans was **Red Ochre People** because of their practice of covering their bodies and belongings with red ochre.

The Beothucks lived in small bands led by chiefs who were skilled hunters. In the warmer months, they lived along the coast. They hunted whales, seals and waterbirds, they fished, and they collected berries, eggs and shellfish. In the fall, they moved inland in larger groups to hunt the caribou. Their bows and arrows, spears, traps and clubs were all made of wood, stone, bone and sinew. Their wigwams were cone-shaped with upstanding tree trunks forming the base and were covered with three layers of birch bark. For transportation in summer, they used birch bark canoes and in winter, they used snowshoes. Their clothing was made from caribou hides sewn together and tied at the waist. Sleeves, leggings, mittens and moccasins were added in colder weather. The many carved bone and ivory pieces found at their burial sites suggest that the Beothuck followed a religion based on belief in spirits.

When the first Europeans arrived in Newfoundland, there were approximately 1000 Beothucks living on the island. It appears they followed a lifestyle very similar to other native peoples in the sub-arctic area of what is now Canada. However, they never established a trading pattern with the Europeans. By the eighteenth century, there were very few remaining Beothuck in Newfoundland. The last of the tribe, Shawnadithit, died in 1829. The Beothuck Indian tribe is now extinct.

Why did this tribe become extinct while others succeeded? What was different about this tribe from all the others in Canada? Why do you think this tribe became extinct when the Micmac tribe moved into the same area and is still thriving on the south coast of the island?

Name: _____

Explorers of Canada

Europeans came to the shores of Canada for two main reasons. First, they were looking for some new land which might bring wealth and glory to the person who discovered it. Second, they were looking for a sea route to the **Indies** which was the general name given to China, Japan and India. Great profits awaited anyone who could find a shorter route than the current one of travelling by land.

After Christopher Columbus discovered what he thought to be India, and Spain had claimed the great quantities of gold to be found there, other monarchs of Europe wanted a share of this new wealth as well. A new reason for exploration arose and soon Portugal, France and England sent out explorers, not only to find a way around the continent which was still in the way of reaching the Indies, but also to claim land and riches for the mother countries.

Do you know strange and unusual facts about these explorers? Read each of the following sentences and circle the correct answer. Use the internet to help you find the information.

1. John Cabot claimed the new found land for England, even though he was:
   a) French.   **b**) Spanish.
   c) Italian.   **d**) Portugese.

2. _____ made the first attempt at establishing an English settlement:
   a) John Cabot   **b**) Martin Frobisher
   c) Simon Fraser   **d**) David Thompson

3. When Martin Frobisher was fourteen he was:
   a) shipwrecked on a voyage to West Africa.   **b**) captured by the Vikings.
   c) graduating from school.   **d**) learning how to sail a ship.

4. _____ also fought against the French at Louisburg, Nova Scotia:
   a) John Cabot   **b**) Samuel de Champlain
   c) Alexander Mackenzie **d**) James Cook

5. Jean Nicollet discovered Lake Superior. Did you know that this explorer:
   a) was very rich?   **b**) did not know how to swim?
   c) was very poor?   **d**) did not like fish?

6. The natives called Nicolas Perrot:
   a) the white man.   **b**) the man from the sea.
   c) the man with the iron legs. **d**) the fur man.

7. Which explorer was killed in Hawaii during a dispute with the natives?
   a) James Cook   **b**) John Cabot
   c) Martin Frobisher   **d**) Henry Hudson

8. Which explorer lived among the natives in the northern fur country for almost 40 years?
   a) David Thompson   **b)** Henry Kelsey
   c) Martin Frobisher   **d)** James Cook

9. Which explorer had an estate called **La Chine**?
   a) Louis Jolliet   **b)** Louis Herrapin
   c) Baron Lahontan   **d)** Cavalier de la Salle

10. Which explorer was never allowed to return to New France?
    a) Louis Herrapin   **b)** Albanel
    c) Jacques Cartier   **d)** Samuel de Champlain

11. Which explorer always took a Chinese cloak with him on his journeys?
    a) Champlain   **b)** Jean de Quen
    c) Jean Nicollet   **d)** Pierre Radisson

12. Baron de Lahontan called Niagara Falls:
    a) falling waters.   **b)** that terrifying cataract.
    c) swift waters.   **d)** the border line.

13. _____ proved that a Northwest Passage did indeed exist:
    a) John Franklin   **b)** Martin Frobisher
    c) David Thompson   **d)** Jacques Cartier

14. _____ officially claimed Newfoundland for England:
    a) John Cabot   **b)** Sir Humphrey Gilbert
    c) Jacques Cartier   **d)** Samuel de Champlain

15. _____ was an English explorer who sailed to the northern part of North America four times:
    a) James Cook   **b)** Alexander Mackenzie
    c) Henry Kelsey   **d)** Henry Hudson

16. _____ was a Canadian explorer who found the Mississippi River in 1673:
    a) Robert de la Salle   **b)** Louis Joliet
    c) Jean Nicollet   **d)** David Thompson

17. _____ was a Scottish born fur trader who charted the Canadian West:
    a) Alexander Mackenzie **b)** Simon Fraser
    b) David Thompson   **d)** Henry Kelsey

18. _____ was a French explorer who was captured by the
    Iroquois:
    a) Jacques Cartier   **b)** Samuel de Champlain
    c) Jean de Quen   **d)** Pierre Radisson

19. _____ surveyed and mapped over 1400 miles of uncharted
    Canadian coastline:
    a) Sir John Franklin   **b)** John Rae
    c) Sir Humphrey Gilbert   **d)** Jacques Cartier

20. _____ had two ships named **Discovery** and **Chatham**:
    a) George Vancouver   **b)** James Cook
    c) Simon Fraser   **d)** Alexander Mackenzie

Answer Key

1. **c) Italian.** Cabot was Italian, but it was the English king who supplied him with the money and ships to make the voyage.

2. **b) Martin Frobisher** - In 1578, Martin Frobisher attempted to start a colony in what is now Nunavut.

3. **a) shipwrecked on a voyage to West Africa.** He was one of only a few survivors.

4. **d) James Cook** - He was an officer in the British navy in 1758, during the siege of Louisburg.

5. **b) did not know how to swim?** He drowned.

6. **c) the man with the iron legs.** They gave him this nickname for his trade of guns for furs.

7. **a) James Cook**

8. **b) Henry Kelsey**

9. **d) Cavalier de la Salle** - He dreamed so much about finding a route to China that his estate was nicknamed La Chine - the French word for China.

10. **a) Louis Herrapin** - He was actually deported from New France.

11. **d) Pierre Radisson** - He always carried a gorgeous Chinese cloak in case he met the emperor of China on one of his voyages.

12. **b) That terrifying cataract.**

13. **a) John Franklin**

14. **b) Sir Humphrey Gilbert**

15. **d) Henry Hudson**

16. **b) Louis Joliet**

17. **a) Alexander Mackenzie**

18. **c) Pierre Radisson**

19. **b) John Rae** - He did this while searching for Sir John Franklin

20. **a) George Vancouver**

Name: _____

Explorers' Word Search

Find the names of the explorers listed below in this puzzle:

```
l a v e r e n d r y e q w e r j t y d h
p g q w e l l i v r e b i d h o e r e u
e t i e n n e b r u l e u y e l t n q m
r r k e l s e y h j k l p i n i o i u p
r e g i j o h n c a b o t f r e k l e h
o h q z m n b v c x z a s d y t o k n r
t s r n w e r t y u i o p l h a o n c e
g i e e s r e i t r a c s e u q c a j y
f b s k d f l z x f v g b h d h n r x g
d o a c t h o m p s o n v b s k m f z i
s r r a m n b v c x z a s d o l k o l l
a f f m w c a l l i d a c h n u j p k b
p i e r r e r a d i s s o n u e a r j e
p h n i a l p m a h c e d l e u m a s r
c a v a l i e r d e l a s a l l e i u t
```

Word List:

Cadillac

Iberville

Fraser

Humphrey Gilbert

Joliet

Perrot

Thompson

Cavalier de la Salle

Etiénne Brule

Frobisher

Jacques Cartier

Kelsey

Pierre Radisson

Cook

Franklin

Henry Hudson

John Cabot

La Verendrye

Samuel de Champlain

Answer Key

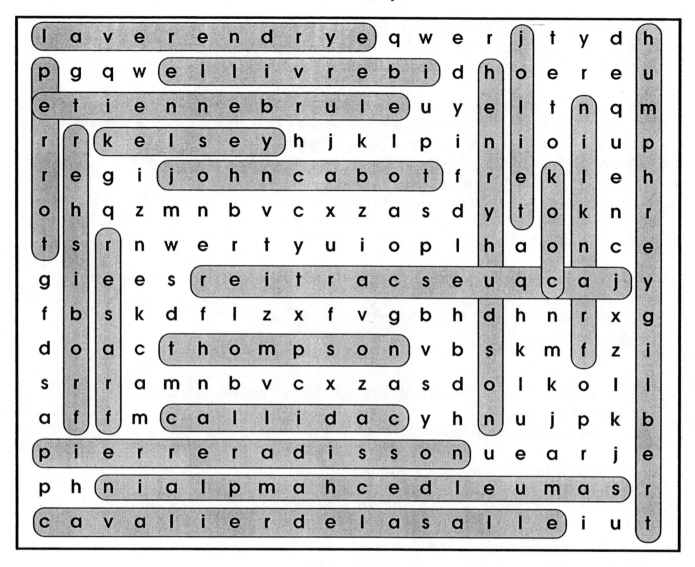

```
l a v e r e n d r y e  q w e r  j  t y d  h
p g q w e l l i v r e b i d h o e r e u
e t i e n n e b r u l e u y e l t n q m
r r k e l s e y h j k l p i n i o i u p
r e g i j o h n c a b o t f r e k l e h
o h q z m n b v c x z a s d y t o k n r
t s r n w e r t y u i o p l h a o n c e
g i e e s r e i t r a c s e u q c a j y
f b s k d f l z x f v g b h d h n r x g
d o a c t h o m p s o n v b s k m f z i
s r r a m n b v c x z a s d o l k o l l
a f f m c a l l i d a c y h n u j p k b
p i e r r e r a d i s s o n u e a r j e
p h n i a l p m a h c e d l e u m a s r
c a v a l i e r d e l a s a l l e i u t
```

Name: _____

Samuel de Champlain

Samuel de Champlain was born in Brouage, France. While he was growing up, he dreamed of being a great explorer. No one in the town guessed that young Samuel would grow up to be one of the great men of his time.

The town of Brouage was a seaport and the men of Samuel's family were captains. He must have heard exciting stories of their travels to foreign lands. Champlain was still a teenager when he went off to war. He served in the French army for several years until peace came in 1598. He went to Spain to learn as much as he could because Spain had more sailors and ships than any other country. He decided that this was the best place to find adventure.

How much do you really know about Samuel de Champlain?

1. Samuel de Champlain's first ocean voyage was to:
    a) North America.   **b)** Mexico.
    c) Africa.   **d)** Ireland.

2. Champlain used these instruments to guide him when he travelled to North America:
    a) the Loran Sea.   **b)** acomputer.
    c) An astrolabe and a compass. **d)** the sun and moon.

3. To amuse his friends, Champlain started the:
    a) Ordre de Bon Temps. **b)** symphony.
    c) Habitation Dancers. **d)** Famille de Nouveau France.

4. One of the favourite meals of Champlain was:
    a) filet mignon.   **b)** rabbit stew.
    c) moose pie.   **d)** apple strudel.

5. Champlain called his settlement in Quebec:
    a) New France.   **b)** the Habitation.
    c) Colony.   **d)** Acadia.

6. Once Champlain reached North America, he preferred to travel by:
    a) snowshoe.   **b)** sled.
    c) toboggan.   **d)** canoe.

7. Beaver pelts were used to make:
    a) coats.   **b)** hats.
    c) boots.   **d)** pies.

8. Champlain crossed the Atlantic between France and New France:
   a) once.   **b)** three times.
   c) 21 times.   **d)** six times.

9. Champlain met the Iroquois Indians dressed in:
   a) a suit of armour.   **b)** skins.
   c) shiny robes.   **d)** white sheets.

10. After the death of Champlain, his wife:
    a) stayed in New France.   **b)** went to Mexico.
    c) became a nun.   **d)** settled in London.

11. Champlain used a gun called the:
    a) pistol.   **b)** arquebus.
    c) rifle.   **d)** long arm.

12. The second Habitation built by Champlain was made of:
    a) wood.   **b)** reeds.
    c) stone   **d)** plywood.

13. The Huron Indians exchanged furs for:
    a) stoves.   **b)** axes.
    c) computers.   **d)** radios.

14. Champlain spent _____ living with the Huron Indians.
    a) two months   **b)** three years
    c) three weeks   **d)** one year

15. Champlain was admired for his skill at:
    a) hunting.   **b)** making maps.
    c) making friends with the Hurons. **d)** cooking.

Answer Key

1. **b) Mexico**. Champlain's first voyage was on a Spanish ship bound for Mexico. He thought it was the most beautiful country in the world.

2. **b) an astrolabe and a compass.** An astrolabe was found near the Ottawa River believed to belong to Champlain. He used it to help him to use the sun and the North Star as his guides.

3. **a) Ordre de Bon Temps.** He created this to keep up the spirits of the people during the long winter months. Each day a different person would be in charge of the meals and each one tried to outdo the others.

4. **c) moose pie**. There were many dishes prepared such as beaver tail, sturgeon, and the meats of the various birds and animals in the area.

5. **b) The Habitation.** It was more like a fort, consisting of four small buildings, all joined together by a high wall.

6. **d) canoe**. He found that the canoes used by the Indians were perfect for the Canadian rivers.

7. **b) hats**. Hatmaking was big business in Europe and the soft fine hairs of the beaver fur were excellent for this.

8. **c) 21 times**

9. **a) a suit of armour.** The arrows didn't penetrate the armour and he frightened them off when he fired his gun.

10. **c) became a nun.** She did not like to live in Quebec and stayed at home in France when Champlain made his last trip across the Atlantic. She joined the Ursulines of Paris in 1645 - ten years after her husband's death.

11. **b) arquebus**. This was a heavy portable gun which fired from the shoulder.

12. **c) stone** - The first Habitation was built of wood.

13. **b) axes**. This was a new tool for them to use in cutting down the trees.

14. **d) one year** - He lived among the Hurons for one year, learning about their life and culture.

15. **b) making maps**. Champlain made maps of all the places he explored in North America.

The Mystery of Oak Island

Oak Island is a small island off the coast of Nova Scotia. It has been the site of the world's longest running treasure hunt in the history of the world. Since its discovery in 1795, millions of dollars have been spent trying to discover what is buried on the island.

One day in 1795, a teenager named Daniel McInnis, was wandering around Oak Island. He noticed a circular depression in the ground under a tree whose branches seemed to have been cut as if they had been used as a pulley. McInnis had heard stories about pirates being seen in the area, so he decided to return to investigate the island.

Over the next several days, McInnis with several of his friends, dug down into the hole. They found a layer of flagstones two feet below the surface and at ten feet a layer of oak logs. The same thing was found at 20 and 30 feet. They could not go any further on their own and decided to leave things as they were until they could return. Eight years later, they came back to the island and continued to dig to a depth of 90 feet. They found a layer of logs at every ten foot interval. Besides the logs, at 40 feet they found a layer of charcoal, at 50 feet a layer of putty and at 60 feet a layer of coconut fibre. At 90 feet they found a stone inscribed with mysterious writing.

After continuing past 90 feet, water began to seep into the pit. By the next day, it was filled with water up to the 33 foot level. Pumping could not keep the water out, so in the following year, a parallel pit was dug down to 100 feet. From there, a tunnel was dug across to the original pit and again water flooded in. After this attempt, the pit on Oak Island was abandoned for 45 years.

In 1849, the Truro Company decided to try to dig up the treasure believed to be buried in the pit. They tried drilling and at 98 feet, a spruce platform was found. Then the drill encountered four inches of oak and 22 inches of what was described as "metal in pieces". Then there were another eight inches of oak, another 22 inches of metal, four inches of oak and another layer of spruce. The company believed it had drilled through two chests filled with coins. The company tried to resume digging the pit in 1850, but again the pit flooded with water. The bottom also fell out of the pit which caused the "treasure" to fall further down into the ground. This time it was discovered that the beach was actually artificial.

Over the next several years different groups of people tried unsuccessfully to build dams, dig more shafts, fill in the drains on the beach and do further drilling. In 1853, a man named Fred Blair decided he would try to excavate the pit. He formed a company called the Oak Island Treasure Company. The pit was drilled to 126 feet where they struck iron. Further down between 150 and 170 feet a cement vault was discovered. When the drill was brought up it had a piece of sheepskin attached to it with letters on it. Even more convinced that a treasure existed, the company sank more shafts into the ground, but still met with failure.

   Over the centuries, and each time someone has decided to recover the treasure from the pit, she/he run into the same problem. The pit floods with water and what has been dug sinks further down, taking the treasure with it. No one has been able to discover what is buried there, who buried it or why. As recent as 1976, a company named Triton dug down to 230 feet and lowered a camera into the hole. The camera showed the image of what appeared to be a severed human hand, three chests, various tools and a human body. Divers were unable to enter the area because of strong currents and poor visibility. Soon after this, the hole collapsed and has not been reopened.

What do you think is buried on Oak Island? Who do you think buried it there?

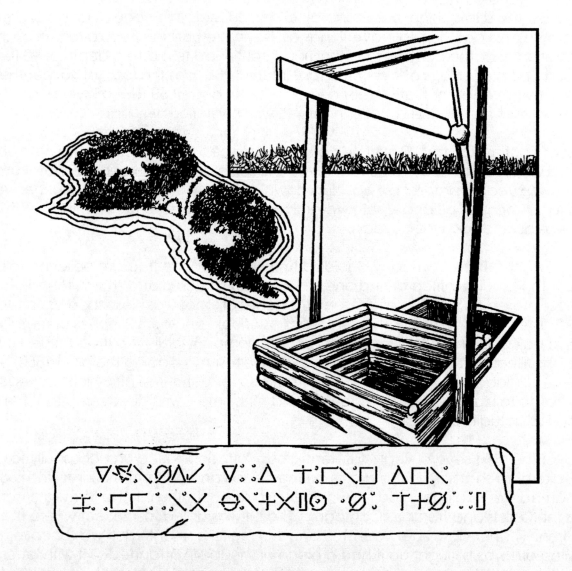

The French and English in Canada

The French were the first to establish settlements in Canada, but were quickly followed by the English who wanted a share of the lucrative fur trade. The French made friends with the Iroquois Indians, while the English were friendly with the Huron Indians. This alliance helped both groups, as there were rivalries between the fierce Iroquois and the peaceful Huron. The French used their influence to encourage the Iroquois to fight the English with them. The French military from France was sent out to keep order in the colony as was the British military, each with orders to prevent the other from gaining control of too much of the new territory.

Two important personalities in Canadian history emerged from this rivalry: Marquis Louis-Joseph de Montcalm and James Wolfe. Montcalm was under orders by the French government to prevent the English from gaining a foothold in New France, while Wolfe was under orders from the English government to drive out the French and take control for Britain. This was the Canadian version of the Seven Years' War which was fought on the other side of the Atlantic. The final battle of this war in Canada was fought on the Plains of Abraham and resulted in ending France's claim to any part of British North America.

How many of these facts about the French and English wars can you answer correctly?

1. Montcalm joined the French army at the age of:
   a) 11.   **b)** 25.
   c) 9.   **d)** 17.

2. He hated the governor of New France because:
   a) he was richer than Montcalm.   **b)** he was born in Canada.
   c) he was born in the same town.   **d)** he was afraid the Indians would attack.

3. Montcalm preferred to fight the English:
   a) like the Indians.   **b)** from the sea.
   c) the way it was done in Europe.   **d)** by hiding inside the fort.

4. Wolfe joined his father's regiment in the British army when he was:
   a) 9.   **b)** 17.
   c) 13.   **d)** 22.

5. Wolfe was very frustrated when he could not defeat the French and:
   a) decided to go back home.   **b)** burned all the countryside.
   c) decided to call a truce.   **d)** sent for reinforcements.

6. The capture of the fortress in Quebec is often referred to as the:
   a) end of an era.   b) Conquest.
   c) revolution.   d) English Rebellion.

7. The region of the St. Lawrence became a British colony called:
   a) Quebec.   b) Lower Canada.
   b) The Province of Quebec. d) English Canada.

8. The Battle of the Plains of Abraham was part of a war between France and England called the:
   a) Seven Years' War.   b) War of the Roses.
   c) American Revolution.   d) Scottish Rebellion.

9. The fighting in the Seven Years' War started in British North America:
   a) as soon as war was declared.   b) two years after war was declared.
   c) two years before war was declared. d) six months after war was declared.

10. The peace treaty which ended the Seven Years' War was the:
    a) Treaty of Ghent.   b) Treaty of Paris
    c) Treaty of Sainte-Foy. d) Treaty of Versailles

11. Under this treaty, the French kept control of:
    a) New Brunswick.   b) Nova Scotia.
    c) Manitoba.   d) St. Pierre and Miquelon.

12. The French were allowed to dry their fish on the:
    a) French Shore of Newfoundland.   b) Gaspe Peninsula of Quebec.
    c) Bay of Fundy Shore.   d) the shores of the St. Lawrence River.

13. The British Admiral who completed the conquest of New France was:
    a) Frederick Carter.   b) Jeffrey Amherst.
    c) Paul Martin.   d) James Pinhorn.

14. Wolfe's second-in-command was:
    a) Paul Martin.   b) Charles Tupper.
    c) Robert Monckton.   d) John Molson.

15. The conquest of New France was completed by the conquest of:
    a) Quebec.   b) Halifax.
    c) Boston.   d) Louisbourg.

Answer Key

1. **c) 9.** - Montcalm joined the French army in 1721 at the age of nine.

2. **b) he was born in Canada.** He regarded the governor, Pierre de Rigaud de Vaudreuil, with contempt because he was born in Canada.

3. **c) the way it was done in Europe.** He did not believe the French should fight the way the Indians fought.

4. **c) 13.**

5. **b) he burned the countryside.** In frustration, when he could not defeat the French, he burned the countryside and ordered the killing of all the habitants.

6. **b) Conquest.** This period in Canadian history has been called "The Conquest of Quebec".

7. **b) the Province of Quebec.**

8. **a) Seven Years' War** - It lasted from 1756 to 1763. It resulted in the end of New France and the beginning of British rule along the St. Lawrence River.

9. **c) two years before war was declared.** The fighting started in British North America in 1754.

10. **b) Treaty of Paris** - It ended the Seven Years' War in 1763.

11. **d)** The islands of **St. Pierre and Miquelon**, off the south coast of Newfoundland, still belong to France.

12. **a) French Shore of Newfoundland.** The French were allowed to land to dry their fish, but were not allowed to settle on the French Shore.

13. **b) Jeffrey Amherst** - He was a British army officer sent to North America in 1758 with orders to capture Louisburg.

14. **c) Monckton** - He was a British army officer posted to Nova Scotia in 1752.

15. **d) Louisburg.** When the French were defeated in Louisburg, it ended the colony known as New France.

Name: _____

Acadians

Acadians is the name given to the French-speaking people in Atlantic Canada. Their ancestors have lived around the Bay of Fundy and the Gulf of St. Lawrence for more than 350 years. Today, Acadian communities are found in all of the Maritime Provinces and also in parts of Quebec. The part of Nova Scotia and New Brunswick where they originally settled was called Acadia. The name came from a mixture of the name given to the area by the 1524 explorer Giovanni da Verrazzano who called it "Arcadie" which refers to a legendary place of beauty and peace and the Micmac name "Cadie" which means sheltered harbour.

The Acadian people were mostly farmers. They raised crops and animals and planted fruit trees. They wanted to remain neutral in the war between France and England. At first the British accepted this position, but later grew suspicious of the growing French population in the region. In 1755, the British decided to get rid of the Acadians. The Acadian people were deported from their homes by the victorious British. Many of them returned to France while some hid in the woods in New Brunswick and Nova Scotia. Some settled on nearby islands and others went to the United States. Large Acadian families were hopelessly separated and many Acadians died during the deportation. The deportation continued until 1762.

How many of these facts about the Acadians and the Deportation can you answer correctly?

1. The Acadians were expelled from their homes because:
   a) they spoke French.   **b)** they refused to take an oath of allegiance to Britain.
   c) hey were good farmers.   **d)** they were Catholic.

2. The Acadian flag has a _____ in one corner.
   a) Face of Mary   **b)** Swastika
   c) star   **d)** ship

3. The Acadian national anthem is:
   a) O Canada.   **b)** Farewell to Nova Scotia.
   c) Stella Maris.   **d)** Fleur de Lys.

4. The Acadians are the ancestors of the:
   a) Scots in Manitoba. **b)** coureurs de bois.
   c) voyageurs.   **d)** Cajuns in Louisiana.

5. It is estimated that about _____ Acadians were deported:
   a) 500   **b)** 10,000
   c) 15,000   **d)** 150,000

6. One group of Acadians spent _____ years in internment camps in England before being sent to France.
   a) 1   **b)** 10
   c) 5   **d)** 7

7. The British officer who expelled the Acadians from the Atlantic region was:
   a) James Wolfe.   **b)** Governor Lawrence.
   c) Governor Phillips.   **d)** Philip d'Entremont.

8. The Acadians were given permission to return in:
   a) 1759.   **b)** 1763.
   c) 1764.   **d)** 1783.

9. The Acadians developed the system of draining the marshes called the:
   a) irrigation system.   **b)** ditching system.
   c) pumping system.   **d)** dyke system.

10. The period of Acadian history from 1600 to 1740 is known as the:
    a) Golden Age.   **b)** Settlement Age.
    c) Shipbuilding Age.   **d)** Farming Age.

11. The Acadians were of the _____ religion.
    a) Anglican   **b)** Catholic
    c) Methodist   **d)** Puritan

12. The first site of Acadian deportation was:
    a) Digby.   **b)** Port Royal.
    c) Grand Pre.   **d)** Moncton.

13. The site of the first deportation is marked today by a:
    a) ship.   **b)** museum.
    c) ibrary.   **d)** cross.

14. The deportation failed in 1762 when _____ refused to accept the Acadians.
    a) Newfoundland   **b)** Massachusetts
    c) Ontario   **d)** Florida

15. When the Acadians returned to Nova Scotia, their farms had been taken over by the English. As a result, many of them decided to move to:
    a) New Brunswick.   **b)** Prince Edward Island.
    c) Newfoundland.   **d)** British Columbia.

Answer Sheet

1. **b) They refused to take an oath of allegiance to Britain.** They preferred to remain neutral and not take an oath of allegiance to Britain because this meant they would have to fight against the French.

2. **a) The Face of Mary.** The Acadian flag which was adopted in 1884 has the French Tricolor, but there is a star "The Face of Mary" situated in the blue rectangle.

3. **c) Stella Maris** is the name of the star on the flag.

4. **d) Cajuns in Louisiana.** Many deported Acadians settled in Louisiana; their ancestors are the Cajuns.

5. **b) 10,000 to 12,000** - Acadians were deported.

6. **d) 7 years.** These people returned to Acadia after twenty years.

7. **b) Governor Lawrence.**

8. **c)** They were allowed to return in **1764**, but still had to swear the oath of allegiance to the British.

9. **d) the dyke system.** They developed an innovative method of turning the salt marshes into farmland by building dykes which prevented the tides from flooding the marshes at high tide, but at the same time allowing the rain water and melting snow to flow out.

10. **a) Golden Age.** This was the age when there were very large families.

11. **b) Catholic** - Family ties and the Catholic religion played a very important part in their lives.

12. **c) Grand Pre.** A monument was erected on the site of the first deportation.

13. **d) cross.**

14. **b) Massachusetts.** The deported Acadians were then returned to Nova Scotia.

15. **a) New Brunswick.** There are over a half a million descendents of these uprooted Acadians living in New Brunswick today.

Name: _____

The Loyalists

The Loyalists were the people who remained loyal to Britain and the British Empire during the American Revolution. During the war, and especially afterwards, thousands of them left the newly formed United States of America and settled in Canada. There were Loyalists in all of the thirteen colonies who came from many different backgrounds. They were rich, poor, slaves, escaped slaves and slave owners, businessmen, farmers, clergymen, soldiers, townspeople and country folk.

The Loyalists were viewed by the Rebels as traitors and were often violently attacked. Loyal families were harassed, driven from their homes, fined, jailed and even killed. The victorious Americans punished those loyal to Britain who tried to remain in their homes. Approximately 45,000 Loyalists came to Canada when they were forced into exile by their former friends.

How much do you really know about the Loyalists in Canada?

1. Every Loyalist who came to Canada was entitled to _____ acres of land.
   a) 400   **b)** 40
   c) 10   **d)** 100

2. The result of Loyalists settling in Nova Scotia was that it was:
   a) unable to provide land for all of them.   **b)** divided into three colonies.
   c) forced to send them to Britain.   **d)** delighted with the arrival of more British.

3. Because of the influx of Loyalists in Nova Scotia, _____ was the largest city in the colony.
   a) Halifax   **b)** Dartmouth
   c) Yarmouth   **d)** Shelbourne

4. The arrival of Loyalists in the St. Lawrence region posed a problem because:
   a) they were Protestant.   **b)** they wanted the best land.
   c) they didn't speak English.   **d)** they wanted to control the government.

5. There were almost 6,000 Loyalist refugees who were:
   a) German.   **b)** of the Six Nations native people.
   c) Dutch.   **d)** French.

6. The Loyalists were seen as _____ in Canada.
   a) traitors   **b)** interlopers
   c) symbols of loyalty   **d)** barbarians

7. The initials, U.E., that were given to Loyalists mean:
   a) Unity of Empire.   **b)** Under Enemy.
   c) Upper Echelon.   **d)** Under Exhaustion.

8. Another name given to the Loyalists was:
   a) Brits.   **b)** Tories.
   c) Shuckers.   **d)** Farmhands.

9. The arrival of the Loyalists marked the beginning of the province of:
   a) Nova Scotia.   **b)** Quebec.
   c) Ontario.   **d)** New Brunswick.

10. The arrival of Loyalists in Canada caused the:
    a) settlement of the West.   **b)** the Red River Rebellion.
    c) the creation of Upper and Lower Canada.   **d)** the Pacific Scandal.

11. Loyalists built the cities of:
    a) St. John and Fredericton.   **b)** Ottawa and Hull.
    c) Oshawa and Whitby.   **d)** New Glasgow and Antigonish.

12. Most of the Loyalists travelled to Canada:
    a) by canoe.   **b)** on foot.
    c) with Indian guides.   **d)** by ship.

13. The Loyalists wanted to make their new country:
    a) a British Empire.   **b)** the envy of the Americans.
    c) a haven for traitors.   **d)** a French-speaking Empire.

14. The treaty which ended the Seven Years' War was:
    a) the Treaty of Paris (1783).   **b)** the Treaty of Paris (1763).
    c) the Treaty of Versailles.   **d)** the Treaty of Peace.

15. The largest influx of Loyalists occurred in 1783, when _____ Loyalists landed in Nova Scotia.
    a) 5,000   **b)** 10,000
    c) 15,000   **d)** 20,000

Answer Key

1. **d) 40.** Every Loyalist who came to Canada was entitled to 100 acres of land. This was approximately 40 hectares.

2. **b) divided into the three colonies.** So many Loyalists arrived in Nova Scotia that in 1784 it divided into Cape Breton, Nova Scotia and New Brunswick.

3. **c) Shelbourne** - For a short time, it had about 8000 people.

4. **a) they were Protestant.** The governor thought there might be problems between the French-speaking Catholics and the English-speaking Protestants.

5. **b) of the Six Nations People.** There were many natives who were loyal to Britain and they lost all their lands in the peace treaty.

6. **c) symbols of loyalty** - They were also seen as symbols of opposition to American democracy and republicanism, and of support for traditional attitudes in society and politics.

7. **a) Unity of Empire.** - These initials were given to Loyalists as a "mark of honour".

8. **c) Tories**

9. **d) New Brunswick.** So many Loyalists arrived that a new colony was created.

10. **c) the Creation of Upper and Lower Canada.** In 1791, the Province of Canada was separated into two provinces: Upper and Lower Canada.

11. **a) St. John and Fredericton.** Loyalists settled along the St. John River and were the largest group of newcomers to the province.

12. **d) by ship.** Fleets of ships brought Loyalists to what are now the Maritime Provinces.

13. **b) the envy of the Americans** "By heaven, we will be the envy of the American states" was a quote from Edward Winslow, one of the leaders of the New Brunswick Loyalists.

14. **a) The Treaty of Paris (1783).** The Treaty of Paris (1763) ended the Seven Years' War.

15. **d) 20,000**

Name: _____

Upper and Lower Canada

In 1791, the Constitution Act divided the old Province of Canada into two colonies: Upper and Lower Canada. Each one was named for its position along the St. Lawrence River. Lower Canada was in the area of present-day Quebec, along the "lower" section of the river. Upper Canada was farther "up" the river. The boundary between the two was the Ottawa River which today separates the provinces of Quebec and Ontario. Both colonies, however, were governed by the British Governor General in Quebec City.

Each colony was given a lieutenant governor, an executive and legislative council, and a legislative assembly. The Act also guaranteed the right of the Roman Catholic Church and the seigneurial system in Lower Canada as well as the French civil laws. The fur trade continued to be as important to Lower Canada as it had been to New France while the economy of Upper Canada continued to depend upon the growing of wheat.

How much do you really know about life in Upper and Lower Canada?

1. In Upper Canada, _____ of all the land was set aside for the purposes of the Anglican Church.
   a) one-fifth   **b)** one-sixth   **c)** one-tenth   **d)** one-seventh

2. The farmers of Lower Canada were called:
   a) habitants.   **b)** Loyalists.   **c)** seigneurs.   **d)** squatters.

3. The English wanted to extend their trade by building _____ on the St. Lawrence River.
   a) bridges   **b)** canals   **c)** locks   **d)** channels

4. The most important activity of the Ottawa River Valley was the:
   a) farming.   **b)** breweries.   **c)** timber trade.   **d)** fur trade.

5. The first job for settlers in Upper Canada was to:
   a) build a log cabin.   **b)** obtain land.
   c) learn the laws.   **d)** join the government.

6. One of the reasons the French in Lower Canada remained loyal to Britain was:
    a) they were afraid the Acadian experience would be repeated.
    b) they were influenced by the priests.
    c) they couldn't speak the language.
    d) they would be put in jail if they weren't.

7. The pioneers in Upper Canada used the ashes left from burning logs to make:
    a) flour.   b) sand.   c) soap.   d) salt.

8. The ashes left from burning logs is called:
    a) potash.   b) kerosene.   c) hash.   d) soot.

9. Governor Simcoe moved the capital of Upper Canada from Newark to York because:
    a) it was easier to get to.   b) the farming was better.
    c) there were more people there.   d) it was too close to the United States.

10. The changing of the forms of government in Upper and Lower Canada came about as a result of:
    a) Confederation.   b) the Riel Rebellion.
    c) The Rebellions of 1837.   d) the American Revolution.

11. The most expensive project ever undertaken in North America by the British was:
    a) the building of the Welland Canal.   b) the building of the Rideau Canal.
    b) the Canadian Pacific Railway.   d) the Grand Trunk Railway.

12. The houses that the seigneurs lived in were called:
    a) maisons.   b) chateaux.   c) castles.   d) cabins.

13. The blacksmith was an important person in the villages of Upper and Lower Canada because he could:
    a) make tools.   b) sell crops.
    c) cut down the trees.   d) speak both languages.

14. The area of Upper Canada was first settled by the:
    a) French.   b) English.   c) natives.   d) Scots.

15. The French population doubled:
    a) every two years.   b) every 25 years.
    c) every six years.   d) every 10 years.

Answer Key

1. **d) one seventh** - The Constitution Act of 1791 set aside one-seventh of the land to be used for the purposes of the Anglican Church and another one-seventh of the land to be used by the Crown to help support the building of roads and other services. This action helped to keep Upper Canada British.

2. **a) habitants.** The French name for the farmers was "habitants" as they rented the land from the seigneurs.

3. **c) canals** - There was a very poor transportation system in Upper Canada.

4. **c) timber trade.** A sawmill was built in Hull and the British increased their demands for Canadian timber.

5. **a) build a log cabin.** The first task faced by newcomers to Upper Canada was to clear the land and build a cabin.

6. **b) they were influenced by the priests.** The Roman Catholic priests were suspicious of the American Protestants and fearful they would be taken over by the United States. As well, the British had let them keep their power in Lower Canada.

7. **c) soap.** Lye was made by leaching water through the ashes. This was added to melted tallow and lard to make soap.

8. **a) potash.**

9. **d) it was too close to the United States.**

10. **c) The Rebellions of 1837.** These rebellions forced the British government to allow responsible government in the colonies.

11. **b) the building of the Rideau Canal.** With its many stone locks and blockhouses, it was the most expensive project of the British in North America.

12. **b) chateaux.** This is the French word for castles.

13. **a) make tools.** Being a blacksmith was the most essential trade since everything depended on the making of tools.

14. **c) natives.** The native peoples who lived in this area were of the Huron, Petun, Neutral and the Algonquin tribes.

15. **b) every 25 years.**

The War of 1812

The War of 1812, which lasted from June 1812 to December 1814, was an important milestone in Canadian history. It was a fight against invasion by the United States. The war was officially between Great Britain and the United States, but because Canada was a British colony next to its border, the Americans decided that a takeover of Canada would drive the British from North America once and for all. Most of the fighting took place along the border between the U.S. and Upper and Lower Canada.

The Americans thought it would be easy to conquer Canada - "just a matter of marching". They expected that the Loyalists who had fled to Canada following the American Revolution would support and welcome the American invasion. They expected the English and the French to rise up and join them to free themselves of British rule. Instead, the settlers fought to retain control of their homeland and remained loyal to the British.

Read each of the following statements and circle the correct answer:

1. The cause of the War of 1812 was:
   a) the Americans were jealous of the Canadians.
   b) the British ships were searching American vessels.
   c) the Americans were searching for escaped slaves.
   d) the Canadians had stolen the American ideas for the timber trade.

2. The war gave captains on the Atlantic Ocean the opportunity to become:
   a) privateers.   b) soldiers.   c) fishermen   d) Canadian citizens.

3. The last major battle of the war was fought on:
   a) Dec.12, 1814.   b) Sept.13, 1814.   c) Oct. 31, 1814.   d) Jan. 8, 1815.

4. The British got their information about where the American troops were from the:
   a) radio.   b) spies.   c) American newspapers.   d) telegraph.

5. One of the battles during the War of 1812 inspired the writing of:
   a) O Canada.   b) the Battle Hymn of the Republic.
   c) the Yellow Rose of Texas.   d) the Star-Spangled Banner.

6. The British army lived mainly on beef:
   a) stolen from the French.   b) smuggled from the United States.
   c) given to them by the natives. d) trapped by the fur traders.

7. Isaac Brock did not want to be in Canada. He wanted to fight against:
    a) Napoleon.   **b)** Hitler.   **c)** De Gaulle.   **d)** Mussolini.

8. Which American city did the British burn in the War of 1812?
    a) Chicago   **b)** Los Angeles   **c)** New Orleans   **d)** Washington

9. The war was nicknamed:
    a) Napoleon's Fancy.   **b)** Canada vs U.S.
    c) Mr. Madison's War.   **d)** The Battle of Niagara.

10. When General Ross died in the Battle of Fort McHenry, the British preserved his body with:
    a) water.   **b)** rum.   **c)** natural preservatives.   **d)** whipped cream.

11. The settlement of _____ was established by the British for black refugees from the War of 1812.
    a) Peterborough   **b)** Oro   **c)** St. Catharine's   **d)** Brockville

12. Laura Secord is considered a heroine of the war because she:
    a) fed chocolate to the soldiers.   **b)** hid the British from the Americans.
    c) walked 30 km to warn the British.   **d)** helped to save Tecumseh.

13. The award Laura received from Queen Victoria in 1860 was:
    a) a gold ring.   **b)** £100.   **c)** a new dress.   **d)** a farm.

14. The close friend and ally of Isaac Brock was:
    a) Tecumseh.   **b)** Proctor.   **c)** Joseph Brant.   **d)** Deerslayer.

15. Which of the following did the Americans gain in the War of 1812?
    a) control of the Niagara Peninsula
    b) unlimited access to Canadian waterways
    c) nothing at all
    d) access to the Canadian West

Answer Key

1. **b) the British ships were searching American vessels.** The British were involved in a war against Napoleon and were enforcing a blockade to prevent any supplies from reaching France.

2. **a) privateers** - The captains of British vessels used the blockade as an opportunity to raid all ships they cam across.

3. **d) Jan. 8, 1815.** The last battle was fought in New Orleans, fifteen days after the war was over.

4. **c) American newspapers.** The American newspapers reported all troop movements and plans of attack.

5. **d) the Star Spangled Banner** - It was during the battle at Fort McHenry that Francis Scott Key wrote the American national anthem.

6. **b) smuggled from the United States.** The beef was smuggled from Maine and Pennsylvania.

7. **a) Napolean.** He wanted to be in Europe and did not like Canada at all.

8. **d) Washington** - In August, 1814, British troops landed near Washington and burned the White House and the Capitol.

9. **c) Mr. Madison's War.** It was nicknamed after President Madison by the people of the Northern States because they did not think he had any reason to declare war.

10. **b) rum.** They kept his body in a barrel of rum to preserve it so they could bring it home to Britain.

11. **b) Oro** - The British encouraged all refugees of the war to become British citizens.

12. **a) walked 30km to warn the British** - She walked from Queenston to Beaver Dam to warn the British that the Americans were planning a surprise attack.

13. **b) £100.** She did not receive this award until she was 85 years old.

14. **a) Tecumseh.** He was a Mohawk who hated the Americans for taking his land in the Ohio Valley.

15. **c) nothing at all.** Both the United States and Canadian territories remained the same after the war.

39

Name: _____

The Reformers and the Durham Report

The Constitution Act created the Province of Canada. However, this did not ensure that everything would go well in the newly formed government. The people in both Upper and Lower Canada were dissatisfied with the power being in the hands of the Governor and his appointed friends. The people still had no real say in how they were governed or in what laws were passed.

In both Canadas, important leaders emerged to fight the British government over the issues. They did not want to go as far as their neighbours to the south had and revolt against British control of the colonies all together. They did want to play a part in how they were governed. This led to the closest Canada has ever come to a civil war.

The Assembly was ridiculed in both parts of the province. This angered the Governor who retaliated against the "Reformers". This did lead to several battles being fought and people losing their lives for what they believed in. One of the French-Canadian leaders was Louis-Joseph Papineau and the English leader in Upper Canada was William Lyon MacKenzie.

Rebellions broke out in both Upper and Lower Canada and many people were killed. The leaders of the rebellion were either arrested or fled to the United States. The British government sent Lord Durham to Canada to investigate the causes of the rebellion and to write a report. He suggested that the two provinces should be united as one with a common government following the system of responsible government.

Answer the following questions about this period of political unrest in Canada by choosing the correct answer.

1. Louis-Joseph Papineau was one of the:
   a) richest men in Paris.   **b)** seigneurs.   **c)** Loyalists.   **d)** fur traders.

2. When Papineau presented the Ninety-Two Resolutions to the British government it took them _____ years to respond:
   a) 6   **b)** 10   **c)** 3   **d)** 2

3. In 1836, a reward of _____ was offered for the capture of Papineau.
   a) $2000.00   **b)** $3000.00   **c)** $6000.00   **d)** $4000.00

4. Papineau made fun of the Assembly and called them the:
   a) Family Compact.   **b)** Snobs.   **c)** Hypocrits.   **d)** Chateau Clique.

5. He was the leader of the:
   a) Patriotes.   **b)** Liberals.   **c)** Conservatives.   **d)** Bleus.

6. After the British army defeated the rebels in Lower Canada, Papineau fled to:
   a) New York.   **b)** Nova Scotia.   **c)** Maine.   **d)** Upper Canada.

7. In 1837, there were race riots in:
   a) Quebec City.   **b)** Montreal.   **c)** Niagara.   **d)** Toronto.

8. On December 5, 1837 _____ was declared in Montreal.
   a) war   **b)** martial law   **c)** revolution   **d)** conscription

9. The leaders of the second rebellion in Lower Canada disguised themselves as:
   a) Indians.   **b)** Americans.   **c)** hunters.   **d)** fishermen.

10. William Lyon Mackenzie won a seat in four by-elections but:
    a) was always prevented from taking his seat.
    b) always refused to sit in the government.
    c) was always the first to show up for meetings.
    d) was always too loud at meetings.

11. He spent _____ in prison for his part in the rebellion of 1837.
    a) 2 years   **b)** 18 months   **c)** 6 days   **d)** 1 year

12. The two reformers who were hanged in public were:
    a) Dr. Charles Duncombe and Peter Matthews
    b) Peter Matthews and Samuel Lount
    c) William Lyon Mackenzie and Louis-Joseph Papineau
    d) Robert Nelson and Samuel Lount

13. The Frères Chausseurs were formed in:
    a) Quebec.   **b)** Ontario.   **c)** the United States.   **d)** Nova Scotia.

14. The reformers defeated the British at the battle of:
    a) St. Denis.   **b)** St. Georges.   **c)** St. Julie.   **d)** Ste. Anne de Beaupre.

15. The first shot fired at Montgomery's Tavern was:
    a) the one that killed Mackenzie.   **b)** a mistake.
    c) the shot that ended the rebellion.   **d)** the one that caused the first World. War.

16. Lord Durham was sent out to Canada to investigate the problems. His nickname in Britain was:
    a) Lord Happy.   **b)** Earl of Canada.
    c) Radical Jack.   **d)** Ireland's Eye.

17. He described Upper and Lower Canada as:
    a) a place fit for kings.
    b) two nations warring in the bosom of one country.
    c) the ends of the world.
    d) a country without government.

18. He called the French-Canadians:
    a) very honest hard-working people.
    b) people who could not speak English.
    c) a group of insignificant farmers.
    d) a people with no history and no literature.

19. His solution for French Canada was:
    a) to assimilate them into the English culture.
    b) to send them back to France.
    c) to try to get them to write French books.
    d) to teach them about history.

20. The recommendations of the Durham Report eventually led to:
    a) revolution.
    b) settling the West.
    c) Confederation.
    d) the building of the C.P.R.

Answer Key

1. **c) seigneurs.** He owned a seigneury at Petite-Nation, Lower Canada.

2. **c) 3** - The British response "The Russell Resolutions" took three years to reach Lower Canada.

3. **d) $4000.00**

4. **d) Chateau Clique.** They were called the Family Compact in Upper Canada.

5. **a) Patriotes.** The party was first called the Canadiens, but later changed its name to the Patriotes.

6. **a) New York.** He lived in Albany, New York for a while before going to France.

7. **c) Niagara.** Two African residents of Niagara were killed and 30-40 others were arrested.

   could be put in jail for no reason.

9. **c) hunters.** They were members of the Freres Chausseurs - rebels who were determined to keep fighting from the United States.

10. **a) was always prevented from taking his seat.** Mackenzie criticized the government so much that even when he was elected by the people, the governor refused to allow him in the legislature.

11. **b) 18 months** - He was arrested and put in prison for violating the neutrality laws between the United States and Britain.

12. **b) Peter Matthews and Samuel Lount.** They were publicly hanged to teach a lesson to the people who opposed the government.

13. **c) The United States.** This organization was formed by rebels who had fled to the United States and intended to attack the British in Lower Canada.

14. **a) St. Denis.** The British were defeated by the rebels after seven hours of fighting.

15. **b) a mistake.** The British commander fired a shot over the heads of the rebels who thought he had fired at them.

16. **c) Radical Jack.** He received this nickname because he was part of the reform wing of the Whig party in England.

17. **b) two nations warring in the bosom of one country.** He saw the French and English Canadians fighting each other for the same things.

18. **d) a people with no history and no literature.**

19. **a) assimilate them into the English culture.** He thought that if the French speaking people could be assimilated into the English culture, the English would be able to rule them.

20. **c) Confederation.** His report led to the union of the two Canadas in 1841, responsible government in 1848 and Confederation in 1867.

Name: _____

The Coming of the Railway

Canada's first railway was the Champlain and St. Lawrence Railroad. It was completed in 1836 and connected La Prairie on the St. Lawrence River with St. Jean on the Richelieu River, a distance of about 80 kilometres. The first railway in the Maritimes was the Albion Mines Railway. This line was completed in 1840 and carried coal from the mines near Pictou, Nova Scotia to the port, a distance of about 9.5 kilometres. The Montreal and Lachine Railroad, completed in 1847, carried goods and passengers from Montreal to Lachine, a distance of about twelve kilometres.

A Guarantee Act of 1849 encouraged investors to put up money needed to finish a railway line between the St. Lawrence River and Portland, Maine. This act also benefitted the Grand Trunk and the Great Western Railway. The Great Western Railway was completed in 1854. This railway ran from Niagara Falls to Windsor. The Grand Trunk Railway was intended to run from the Great Lakes to the Atlantic Ocean. The Canadian Pacific Railway which connected British Columbia to the rest of Canada was the most ambitious railroad project in Canada. It resulted in the settlement of Western Canada and many towns sprang up alongside the railroad tracks to serve as distribution centres.

Read the following amazing facts about railways in Canada. Circle the letter of the correct answer for each statement.

1. The first steam engine to roll along railroad tracks in Canada was called the:
   a) Train.   **b)** Kitten.   **c)** Rail.   **d)** Car.

2. The first locomotive in Canada to burn coal and run on all iron tracks was called the:
   a) Kitten.   **b)** Train.   **c)** Samson.   **d)** Walleye.

3. One of the first passengers on the railway in Canada was:
   a) the Prime Minister.   **b)** the Governor.
   c) the owner of the railway.   **d)** the bride of the Governor General.

4. Railway shares in the 1850s were bought with:
   a) money.   **b)** butter, eggs and meat.   **c)** land.   **d)** timber.

5. In the Guarantee Act of 1849, the Canadian government agreed to pay:
   a) 6% interest on bonds.   **b)** 10% interest on bonds.
   c) 2% interest on bonds.   **d)** 5% interest on bonds.

6. The railway schemes of the 1850s resulted in:
   a) railroads not being used.   **b)** the Bank of Canada going bankrupt.
   c) the governor resigning.   **d)** the resignation of the Assembly.

7. As each section of the Grand Trunk Railway was opened:
   a) a toll bridge was torn down.   **b)** a new railway was started.
   c) a carnival was held.   **d)** another road was destroyed.

8. The first train to travel on the Peterborough-Coburg Line went at a speed of:
   a) 15 miles an hour.   **b)** 60 miles an hour.
   c) 100 miles an hour.   **d)** 20 miles an hour.

9. Wooden tracks topped with flat iron that curled up in the summer time were called:
   a) woodsies.   **b)** arrests.   **c)** snake rails.   **d)** stop and go rails.

10. The first iron railway locomotive was nicknamed the:
    a) Iron Horse.   **b)** Steamy.   **c)** Smokey.   **d)** Ironsides.

11. The completion of the Canadian Pacific Railway was:
    a) intended to bring Newfoundland into Confederation.
    b) intended to help annex the western part of the United States.
    c) a condition of British Columbia entering Confederation.
    d) originally intended to go to Dawson City.

12. The Canadian Pacific Railway was the _____ railway in the world.
    a) shortest   **b)** most expensive   **c)** cheapest   **d)** longest

13. By 1915, there were _____ railways going across Canada.
    a) 2   **b)** 3   **c)** 4   **d)** 5

14. All the railroads in Canada were combined to form the:
    a) Grand Trunk Railway   **b)** Canadian Pacific Railway
    c) Canadian Northern Railway   **d)** Canadian National Railway

15. Since the 1960s, trains have been powered by:
    a) coal.   **b)** oil.   **c)** diesel.   **d)** wood.

Answer Key

1. **b) Kitten.** The Kitten, a balky little steam engine built in England and assembled in Montreal, made her debut in Canada.

2. **c) Samson.** The Samson could pull 32 cars up a steep hill.

3. **d) the bride of the Governor General.** The car became known as the "Bride's Coach".

4. **b) butter, eggs and meat.** Farmers in the townships bought shares in the railroad with food needed for the construction gangs.

5. **a) 6% interest on bonds.** The government agreed to pay 6% interest on bonds of any railway over 75 miles long. This assured investors of a return on their money before the line was completed.

6. **b) the Bank of Canada going bankrupt.** The failure of the Bank of Canada is attributed to the misuse of public funds and the politicians' railway schemes.

7. **b) a carnival was held.** A civic carnival was used to mark each triumph.

8. **a) 15 miles an hour.**

9. **c) snake trails.** They twisted and rose in the heat of the summer.

10. **a) Iron Horse.** This was the "Lady Elgin" - the first locomotive for the Ontario, Simcoe and Huron Railway.

11. **a) a condition of British Columbia entering Confederation.**

12. **d) longest**

13. **b) 3** - They were the Grand Trunk, the Canadian Pacific and the Canadian Northern.

14. **d) Canadian National Railway.** All the railways were in financial trouble trying to compete with one another. The government bought them all.

15. **c) diesel.** This is the cheapest form of fuel for trains.

A Mystery From History

The Franklin Expedition

John Franklin was born in Spilsby, Lincolnshire, England in 1786. Explorers were searching for a sea route from the Atlantic to the Pacific through the icy waters of the Arctic Ocean. Franklin joined the Royal Navy when he was fifteen years old. He made four Arctic voyages and mapped 1200 miles of coastline. During his second expedition, he and his crew almost starved to death. Although some of the crew died, those who survived did so by chewing on anything they could find that had any possible nutritional value - even their own leather boots. When they returned to Britain with the tales of their latest expedition they became heroes. Franklin was given a knighthood and a new expedition was arranged in 1845 to map the missing pieces of the Northwest Passage.

On May 19,1845, Franklin with officers and crew totaling one hundred and thirty-five men set sail in two iron-fortified ships named the Terror and the Erebus. Their last confirmed sighting was two months later in Baffin Bay. What happened to them after that remains a mystery.

When no word had been received from the ships by 1847, other expeditions were sent out in search of the missing ships. Dozens returned without finding a trace of them In 1850, clues to their fate were found. The graves of three crew members were discovered on Beechey Island along with a number of tins that indicated the crews had spent a winter in the area. Four years later, a surveyor, John Rae, obtained information from a group of Inuit hunters that the crews had abandoned the expedition. They had headed south after being locked in by the ice. They gave him engraved spoons as proof that what they were saying was the truth.

In 1858, Franklin's wife, Lady Jane Franklin, funded an expedition of her own to find her husband. On King William Island, the captain, Leopold McClintock, discovered a gruesome scene. There were headless skeletons lying in the snow and a boat was tied to a sled. The items aboard the boat were very impractical for people living this far north - combs, slippers, and a novel. In a stone cairn nearby, two notes were found: one dated May 28, 1847 which said "All Well" and another dated April 25, 1848 detailing the abandonment of the ship, Franklin's death, as well as that of 24 crew members. The second note also told of the survivors' intent to travel south to Black Fish River.

What do you think happened to these men?

What do you think Franklin and the crew died from?

Name: _____

The Dawn of Confederation

During the 1860s when politics was the leading issue among those who were politically inclined, there were other issues which took up the time of the ordinary people. The Canadian people lived much as they had before the Rebellions of 1837, Lord Durham's report and responsible government. Their lives were very much tied in with loyalty to Britain and all things British. They had a dislike and mistrust of the Atlantic colonies and did not give much thought at all to the largely unknown Northwest. Even the exciting news of the discovery of gold in the West only stirred them mildly. Approximately 80 per cent of the population lived in rural and isolated areas - on farms, in lumber camps, in sea-coast villages. The country's major industries were connected with the forests, the farms and the sea.

With the threats of war in the United States and Mexico, British North America seemed like a haven of peace and tranquility. However, a sense of unease began to creep in. The fear of being annexed to the United States, the raids by groups of Irish called the Fenians, and the loss of the free trade with the British colonies forced Canadians to take a second look at their political situation.

How did the ordinary person in Canada live during these turbulent times? What were their favourite forms of enjoyment?

1. In the 1860s, the British North American colonies were planning a union because:
   a) they wanted to talk about Confederation
   b) the son of Queen Victoria was coming to visit
   c) they wanted to join the South in the American Civil War
   d) they wanted to move further west.

2. Albert, the consort of Queen Victoria introduced the _____ to Nova Scotia.
   a) steamship   **b)** fur-lined boot
   c) Christmas tree   **d)** cobblestone streets

3. The Toronto journalists were angry that the Prince of Wales:
   a) did not talk to them   **b)** danced and partied
   c) could understand French   **d)** did not like Canada

4. The Prince of Wales was the first to play _____ at Niagara Falls.
   a) hockey   **b)** 10-pin bowling
   c) baseball   **d)** basketball

5. On board the steamer, Queen Victoria, John A. Macdonald spent _____ on champagne to try to win over those who opposed Confederation.
   a) $500.00   **b)** $13,000.00
   c) $6500.00   **d)** $2000.00

6. In Charlottetown, the delegation from New Brunswick slept:
   a) in a hotel   **b)** aboard the steamship
   c) in an oyster bar   **d)** on the street

7. Joseph Howe of Nova Scotia called the idea of Confederation a:
   a) botheration   **b)** catastrophe
   c) tragedy   **d)** necessary evil

8. At the Charlottetown Conference, Christopher Dunken talked for _____ against the idea of Confederation.
   a) two hours   **b)** three days
   c) four hours   **d)** two days

9. The Quebec Resolutions were approved at:
   a) 6:00 p.m.   **b)** 4:00 p.m.
   c) 4:30 a.m.   **d)** 6:30 a.m.

10. On the way home from Charlottetown on Derby Day, Cartier and Galt threw _____ at each other.
    a) bags of flour   **b)** eggs
    c) rocks   **d)** potatoes

11. The original idea for the Atlantic colonies in Confederation was to:
    a) not allow them to join   **b)** let them form their own country
    c) make all the people move to Canada West **d)** form one big Eastern province

12. John A. Macdonald described George Etiénne Cartier as:
    a) a short fat man   **b)** a Montrealer, body and soul
    c) a sassy French-Canadian **d)** a terrible editor

13. George Brown waited until midnight to write of Confederation in his paper because:
    a) he preferred to write in the morning
    b) he didn't want to work on Sunday
    c) he was afraid the people would change their minds
    d) he didn't know what to write

14. The wives of the politicians at Charlottetown have been called:
    a) Poor Little Women   **b)** The Forgotten Canadians
    c) The Secret Society **d)** The Mothers of Confederation

Answer Key

1. **b) The son of Queen Victoria.** The Prince of Wales was coming to British North America for a royal visit.

2. **c) Christmas tree** - He called it by the German name "tannenbaum".

3. **c) could understand French.** They were angry that he appeared to enjoy the long speeches that were given by the French-Canadian politicians.

4. **b) 10-pin bowling** - Previously, only nine-pin bowling had been played.

5. **b) $13,000.00** - Magnificent balls and feasts were held aboard the steamship to try to sway those opposed to Confederation.

6. **c) in an oyster bar.** The town was filled with people to see the circus and no one had made reservations for the delegates.

7. **a) botheration.** He did not think anyone would take this idea seriously.

8. **d) two days** - Each person had to be allowed to speak as long as he liked in order that no one could complain about not being allowed to speak their piece.

9. **c) 4:30 a.m.** - It was Saturday, March 11.

10. **a) bags of flour** - This supplied comic relief to the spectators on Derby Day.

11. **d) form one big Eastern province.** This was the original idea because the Maritime colonies had financial problems.

12. **b) a Montrealer, body and soul.**

13. **c) He didn't want to work on Sunday.** He didn't want to profane the Sabbath.

14. **d) The Mothers of Confederation.**

John A. Macdonald

   John Alexander Macdonald was born in Glasgow, Scotland on January 11, 1815. When he was five, he moved to Upper Canada with his family. They settled in the Kingston area. His father was a shopkeeper, but not a very good businessman, so the family was not very well off. His mother worried more about money than his father did and it was she who held the family together and managed its affairs.

   She was determined that John was to have a good education. He attended school in Kingston, where he studied Latin, French, mathematics, history and other subjects. At age fifteen, he was apprenticed to become a lawyer in the office of George MacKenzie. By the time John was seventeen, he was taking charge of the law office in Napanee. He soon earned a reputation of being a hardworking honest lawyer and had many clients.

   John became involved in politics during the Rebellion of 1837, when he joined the militia against William Lyon Mackenzie King. He continued his interest and became part of the government of Canada West. He was co-leader of the Canadas with George Brown and became an avid supporter of Confederation. He was instrumental in having the Seventy-Two Resolutions passed in Charlottetown and later in London. When Confederation became a reality, John A. Macdonald became the first Prime Minister of Canada.

There are a lot of things about John A. Macdonald's life that are amazing. How many of the following things do you know about him?

1. In school, John A. Macdonald was a:
    a) high school athlete   **b)** bookworm   **c)** great debater   **d)** teacher's pet

2. The girls called John A. Macdonald:
    a) Handsome Mac   **b)** Talking Mac
    c) Ugly John Macdonald   **d)** Wee Willie Winkle

3. His mother decided he should become a lawyer because:
    a) that was the cheapest education   **b)** he couldn't do anything else
    c) she had always wanted to be a lawyer   **d)** he was a good writer

4. In Napanee, George MacKenzie noticed that John A. Macdonald:
    a) spent too much time with the girls   **b)** drank too much coffee
    c) spent too much time alone   **d)** did not do his work properly

5. At John's first court case, he:
    a) lost the case   **b)** got into a fist fight   **c)** won the case   **d)** was too scared to talk

6. John A. Macdonald had an excellent:
    a) ability to skate   **b)** ability to eat   **c)** memory   **d)** ability to talk

7. John A. Macdonald's wife, Isabella:
    a) was six years older than him   **b)** was six years younger than him
    c) was the same age as him   **d)** was two years younger than him

8. At the time, _____ was the capital of the Canadas.
    a) Toronto   **b)** Montreal   **c)** Kingston   **d)** Ottawa

9. John A. Macdonald wrote _____ of the Seventy-Two Resolutions.
    a) none   **b)** 10   **c)** 62   **d)** 50

10. John's second wife, Agnes, was often called:
    a) the stepmom   **b)** John's second
    c) Macdonald's good angel   **d)** the English woman

11. When the Dominion of Canada was created, Queen Victoria made John A.
    Macdonald a:
    a) knight   **b)** new hat   **c)** new coat   **d)** crown

12. John and Agnes talked to each other in Parliament by:
    a) telephone   **b)** walkie-talkie   **c)** sign language   **d)** blowing kisses

13. To keep order in the West, MacDonald created the:
    a) Secret Service   **b)** FBI   **c)** CIA   **d)** RCMP

14. Many people have called John A. Macdonald:
    a) The Old Geyser   **b)** The Old Chieftain
    c) Canadian Knight   **d)** Bah Humbug

15. When John A. MacDonald died, railway stations were draped in:
    a) red and white   **b)** blue and black
    c) yellow and green   **d)** purple and black

16. He was taken to his final resting place in a:
    a) car   **b)** limousine
    c) CPR train   **d)** steamboat

Answer Key

1. **b) bookworm**. He loved books and read everything he could.

2. **c) Ugly John Macdonald.** He had frizzy hair and a long bumpy nose which gave his face an almost comical look.

3. **a) that was the cheapest education.** In those days, a lawyer started off by working as an apprentice.

4. **c) spent too much time alone.** He thought that people might not feel comfortable with a quiet lawyer and told him to get out more.

5. **b) got into a fist fight.** He punched the Crown Prosecutor in the nose.

6. **c) memory.** He could remember everything about everyone he met.

7. **a) was six years older than him.** People were doubtful that the marriage would last, but it was a happy one.

8. **c) Kingston** - This was great as he worked in the city.

9. **d) 50** - He was committed to the idea of Confederation.

10. **c) Macdonald's good angel.** She decided that her husband needed looking after.

11. **a) knight.** He became Sir John A. Macdonald.

12. **c) sign language.** They learned sign language so they could talk to each other during the proceedings in the House.

13. **d) RCMP.** He created the Royal Canadian Mounted Police.

14. **b) The Old Chieftain.**

15. **d) purple and black.**

16. **c) CPR train.**

A Mystery From History

The Mystery of the Mary Celeste

One of the great maritime mysteries of Nova Scotia is that of the sailing ship - the Mary Celeste. Over 125 years ago, the ship was found floating, crewless, in the middle of the Atlantic Ocean, in apparent pristine condition. The fate of the crew and the passengers has never been explained.

The Mary Celeste was launched in 1861, from the farmyard at Spencer's Island near the head of the Bay of Fundy, under the name Amazon. The ship was accidentally grounded at Cow Bay in Cape Breton in 1868, after which she was repaired and renamed the Mary Celeste. She operated under an American flag out of New York.

On November 7, 1872, the Mary Celeste sailed under the command of Captain Benjamin Briggs bound for Europe with a cargo of wines and liquors. He was accompanied by his wife, his young daughter and a crew of seven men.

On December 4, 1872, the Mary Celeste was found floating 600 miles off Gibraltar. The official report stated that everything seemed to be in order, except that the ship's paper and chronometer were missing. The last entry in the captain's log was dated November 24 and gave no indication that anything unusual was happening.

There were several reports of the finding of the ship at the time and each one reported different conditions regarding its condition. One report suggested that there was blood on some of the sails and that bloodied weapons were found aboard. This has led some people to think that the ship was attacked by pirates, but does not explain why the money box and cargo was untouched. Another report stated that the lifeboat was still strapped to the ship.

Over the years there have been many theories put forward to explain the strange findings including:

- the crew and passengers may have been swept overboard by a large wave.
- the captain was part of a plot to apply for salvage rights to the abandoned ship.

What is the real story of the Mary Celeste? Write what you think may have happened.

Gold Fever

During the second half of the nineteenth century, tens of thousands of people flocked to British Columbia and the Yukon hoping to strike it rich. Gold was discovered in the Fraser River Valley in 1856 and in the Cariboo Mountains between 1860 and 1866. Many towns and cities sprung up overnight with the large influx of people from all over the world.

Gold had been found in the Canadian North before these dates but it required special skills and machinery to extract it from the ground. The gold that sparked the rushes was found in the streams and rivers. It was known as "placer" or "alluvial" gold. No special training or equipment was needed and anyone with a spirit of adventure and determination had a chance of striking it rich.

The native people unwittingly started the gold rush in the Fraser River Valley. They discovered the gold and sold it to the Hudson Bay Company. When the company sent the gold to the mint in San Francisco, news spread rapidly that there were tremendous amounts of gold just waiting for miners. The Cariboo Gold Rush was much larger than the Fraser River Gold Rush and led people to believe that much larger amounts of gold could be found farther North. This resulted in large areas of the Canadian North being opened for settlement, as well as the creation of the province of British Columbia and the Northwest Territories.

Read each of these facts about the gold rushes and circle the letter before the correct answer.

1. The largest city west of Chicago and north of San Francisco in 1858 was:
   a) Vancouver   **b)** Yale   **c)** Whitehorse   **d)** Victoria

2. The Overland Trail was really made up of _____ sections of road.
   a) 5   **b)** 6   **c)** 2   **d)** 3

3. The founder of Dawson City was Joseph Ladue who was born in:
   a) Ottawa, Ontario   **b)** San Francisco, California
   c) Schuyler, New York   **d)** Vancouver, British Columbia

4. Jim Wallwork was known for:
   a) finding the first gold mine   **b)** first setting foot in Alaska
   c) hauling a steamboat over the mountains   **d)** making friends with the Eskimo

5. The first woman to walk into the North was given the nickname:
    a) Walking Woman   **b)** Klondike Kate
    c) Canadian Cathy   **d)** Northern Nancy

6. There were _____ people who set out for the Klondike Gold Rush from the Red River Valley.
    a) 60   **b)** 150   **c)** 55   **d)** 1000

7. Jack London, who wrote <u>White Fang</u>, was also:
    a) a miner   **b)** a Mountie
    c) a native Indian   **d)** a politician

8. Most miners averaged between:
    a) $15 - $20 a day   **b)** $8 - $13 a day
    c) $150 - $200 a day   **d)** $800 - $1300 a day

9. On the gold fields, a barrel of flour cost:
    a) $100.00   **b)** $20.00   **c)** $10.00   **d)** $50.00

10. The army banished the _____ from the goldfields for a month:
    a) Americans   **b)** Eskimo
    c) Negroes   **d)** Chinese

11. The amount of gold that a miner owned was called his:
    a) income   **b)** poke
    c) claim   **d)** fortune

12. A sourdough was the name given to:
    a) an old, experienced miner   **b)** a moldy piece of bread
    c) a low hill   **d)** a crooked person

13. The people who walked to the gold fields were called:
    a) foolish   **b)** walkers
    c) Overlanders   **d)** Klondikers

14. The term given to looking for gold in the rivers was:
    a) fishing   **b)** paddling
    c) rooting   **d)** panning

15. The miners who first arrived at the gold fields were called:
    a) Johnny Come Latelys   **b)** New Ones
    c) Greenhorns   **d)** Prospectors

Answer Key

1. **b) Yale.**

2. **a) 5** - The Overland Trail was made up of five sections of road divided by four rivers.

3. **c) Schuyler, New York.**

4. **c) hauling a steamboat over the mountains.** He hauled a steamboat named Daisy over the mountains from Edmonton to Dawson City.

5. **b) Klondike Kate.** Kathleen Eloisa Rockwell was the first woman to walk into the North over the rugged Stikine Trail. She was also the first female Royal Canadian Mounted Police Officer.

6. **d) 150** - The main party of the Overlanders consisted of about 150 people from the Red River Valley.

7. **a) a miner.** He didn't make a fortune in the goldfields, but he did write several books about the North.

8. **b) $8-$13 a day.** Even though reports said otherwise, many miners did not make a lot of money.

9. **a) $100.00.** The costs of everything rose dramatically in the towns and cities that sprung up.

10. **d) Chinese** - The Chinese were banished from the gold fields because it was believed they gave supplies to the Indians who attacked the miners.

11. **b) poke.** This is because the miners carried their gold in a pouch called a poke.

12. **a) sourdough.**

13. **c) Overlanders.** They were given this name because they walked over land from Red River.

14. **d) panning.** They dipped up pans of water and gravel and sluiced the water out to leave the gold nuggets.

15. **c) Greenhorns.**

Gold Rush Puzzle

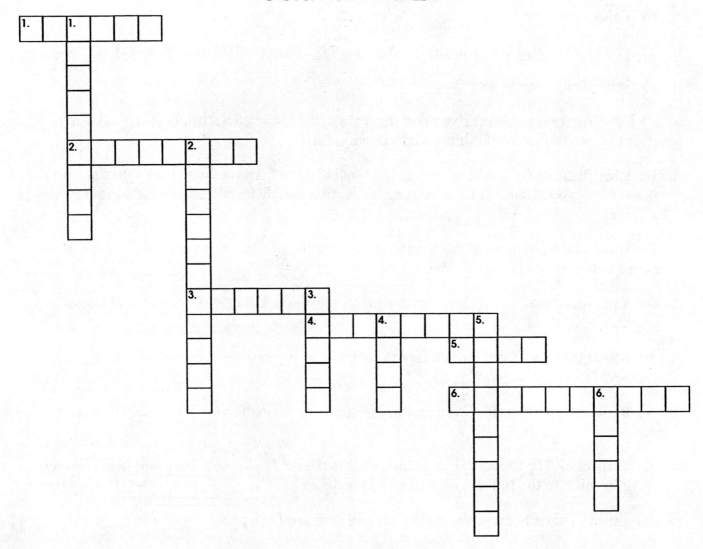

Across:
1. a lump of gold
2. any place rich in gold
3. gold in very small bits
4. the waste left from mining
5. the amount of nuggets a miner owns
6. a person who searches for metals

Down:
1. the excitement and rush to the gold lds
2. a place where the gold was evaluated
3. a wooden peg driven into the ground
4. a vein of gold
5. an old experienced miner
6. a piece of land owned by a miner

The Alaska Boundary Dispute

Alaska was once owned by Russia who had established fur trading bases at places such as Petersburg and Wrangell. This right was confirmed in a treaty with Great Britain in 1825. The United States purchased Alaska from Russia in 1867 and took possession of whatever maps the Russians had that showed what they believed to Alaska. However, the Russian maps showed much more territory than was detailed in the treaty of 1825, which set the boundary.

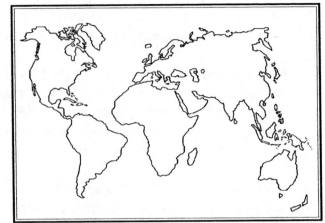

In 1872, British Columbia had become a province of Canada and wanted to set its own boundaries. It petitioned the United States for an official survey of the boundary. The United States dismissed the request saying it was too expensive for them to bother with. In 1898, a high commission met to decide on the boundary dispute and both sides agreed to a compromise. However, the news of this compromise leaked out and the western states caused such an uproar that the United States was forced to forget the compromise. Later that same year, Britain and the United States met to decide on a tribunal to settle the dispute. They could not reach a decision either and the discussions were stopped.

Canadian miners in Alaska were denied certain rights because of a loophole in the Alaskan Homestead Act of 1899. The Americans also started settlements along the southern Panhandle border. The final harassment was policy and unofficially adopted which saw the United States deliberately slowing down Canadian shipments and speeding up the American shipments.

In January 1903, Britain and the United States formally agreed to address the issue. Each side would select three impartial judges of repute. Legal teams would present their cases to these judges and a decision would be made. President Roosevelt appointed three judges with a warning that if they did not find in favour of the United States, he would send in the Marines to secure the rights of the Americans.

Britain appointed two Canadian judges and one British judge. Canada was confident that the British judge would rule in favour of Canada. After weeks of discussion and pouring over documents, a decision was made. The British judge agreed with the Americans. The Alaskan Boundary dispute was over and finalized on paper. This decision has never been challenged by either Canada or the United States.

Why do you think the British judge sided with the Americans?

Name: _____

Confederation of Canada

The original Canadian provinces were Ontario, Quebec, Nova Scotia and New Brunswick. Prince Edward Island and Newfoundland did not join in 1867 because they did not see any benefit to such a union. As the West was gradually opened up for settlement, new provinces were formed and by the turn of the century, Canada stretched from sea to sea. Newfoundland did not join Confederation until 1949.

It was not an easy decision in all of the country to join forces with Central Canada. There were many disagreements, long drawn out arguments and battles before consensus was finally reached. In Manitoba, this meant open rebellion against the authority of Ottawa. It led to the establishment of the R.C.M.P. to keep law and order in the West and the completion of the C.P.R.

Check your knowledge of Canadian Confederation by circling the correct answer to complete each of the following statements:

1. Manitoba was once called the:
   a) postage-stamp province   b) Riel's Land
   b) Gitche Manitou   d) The Land God Gave to Cain

2. When the province of Manitoba was created, it consisted of:
   a) all of the West   b) part of Ontario
   c) only the settled area around Winnipeg d) part of Saskatchewan

3. In the Northwest Territories, the Crown Land is owned by:
   a) the territorial government   b) the Inuit
   c) The Dene Nation   d) the federal government

4. The ordinary members in a territorial government become the:
   a) Cabinet Ministers   b) unofficial opposition
   c) Executive Council   d) Members of Parliament

5. British Columbia did not enter Confederation in 1867 because:
   a) the people did not know anything about Upper and Lower Canada
   b) the people did not want to have anything to do with the Maritimes
   c) the Governor did not approve of Confederation
   d) the people thought they would lose all their gold to central Canada

6. Prince Edward Island has been called:
   a) the cradle of civilization   b) the unwanted island
   c) the little island   d) Red Island

7. Most of the land on Prince Edward Island was owned by:
   a) the government   **b)** slaves
   c) absentee landlords   **d)** politicians

8. The word "Yukon" means:
   a) you can come   **b)** young Canada
   c) you must go   **d)** great river

9. When Saskatchewan and Alberta were made provinces of Canada, they were not given:
   a) control of the land   **b)** the right to vote
   c) the power to make laws **d)** the right to collect taxes

10. Newfoundland did not join Confederation in 1867 because:
    a) the people thought they would not be allowed to catch any more fish
    b) the people thought they would have to pay higher taxes
    c) the people did not know where Canada was
    d) the people wanted a road built to Nova Scotia

11. In the new territory of Nunavut,:
    a) the Inuit must have a percentage of all government jobs
    b) the Inuit are not allowed to hold government jobs
    c) no English speaking people are allowed
    d) everyone must follow the native way of life

12. In the territories, the Canadian government is allowed to:
    a) tell everyone to leave at any time
    b) interfere with education
    c) interfere with the elections
    d) cancel all forms of native privileges

13. In Manitoba, Louis Riel set up a:
    a) provincial government   **b)** federal government
    c) municipal government   **d)** provisional government

14. In the 1950s the Canadian government persuaded the Inuit of Nunavut to:
    a) start their own country **b)** abandon their traditional way of life
    b) move to Ontario   **d)** move farther south

15. Newfoundland entered Confederation because of a(n):
    a) election   **b)** law passed in Britain
    c) referendum   **d)** person who lied to the government

Answer Key

1. **a) postage-stamp province.** It received this name because its size and shape was similar to a postage stamp.

2. **c) only the settled area around Winnipeg.** The rest of the area was known as the Northwest Territories.

3. **d) the federal government**. They are held by the federal government in Ottawa for the Crown. In a province, they are owned by the provincial government.

4. **b) unofficial opposition**. They are responsible for making the government accountable and responsive to the people.

5. **c) the governor did not approve of Confederation.** The governor of the colony at that time was Governor Seymour and he opposed Confederation.

6. **a) the cradle of civilization**. It was here that the idea of Confederation was first proposed.

7. **c) absentee landlords**. Most of the land on the island was owned by people who lived in England and rented the land to the farmers.

8. **d) great river.** It is named for the Yukon River which flows through it.

9. **a) control of the land**. This control was not passed over to the provinces until 1925 in Alberta and 1930 in Saskatchewan.

10. **b) people thought they would have to pay higher taxes**. They were told this by the anti-Confederate, Charles Fox Bennett.

11. **a) the Inuit must have a percentage of all government jobs.**

12. **b) interfere with education.** The federal Parliament can interfere with the school curriculum.

13. **d) provisional government.** The purpose of this government was to negotiate the terms under which Manitoba would join Confederation.

14. **b) abandon their traditional way of life**. They were persuaded to give up their nomadic form of life and move into permanent settlements.

15. **c) referendum**

The Naming of the Capital Cities

The capital city of Canada is Ottawa, Ontario. Each province and territory also has its own capital city.

- Newfoundland - St. John's
- Prince Edward Island - Charlottetown
- Nova Scotia - Halifax
- New Brunswick - Fredericton
- Quebec - Quebec City
- Ontario - Toronto
- Manitoba - Winnipeg

- Saskatchewan - Regina
- Alberta - Edmonton
- British Columbia - Victoria
- Nunavut - Iqaluit
- Northwest Territories - Yellowknife
- Yukon - Whitehorse

How much do you really know about the capital cities of Canada and how they got their names?

1. Ottawa used to be called:
   a) York
   c) Bytown
   b) Kingstown
   d) Hochelaga

2. The word "Ottawa" means:
   a) river
   c) native
   b) trade
   d) young

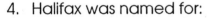

3. St. John's, Newfoundland was named for:
   a) John Efford
   c) St. John the Baptist
   b) John White
   d) John Deere

4. Halifax was named for:
   a) Hal Hayes
   c) Harold of Normandy
   b) George Montagu Dunk
   d) Hail to the Chief

5. The capital of New Brunswick was originally called:
   a) King Frederick
   c) Fred's Town
   b) Fredericktown
   d) Frederick's Burrough

6. Charlottetown received its name from:
   a) Queen Victoria's daughter
   c) the niece of the mayor
   b) the wife of King George III
   d) the name of the first ship to the island

7. The word "Quebec" means:
   a) land of the French
   c) narrow river
   b) new land
   d) falling waters

8. The name of Toronto was first used by:
    a) Jacques Cartier   **b)** Champlain
    c) John A. Macdonald   **d)** Mackenzie King

9. The word "Toronto" means:
    a) trees standing in water **b)** way to the west
    c) way to the east   **d)** end of the river

10. "Winnipeg" is a Cree word meaning:
    a) wooden leg   **b)** dirty water
    c) flat land   **d)** no trees

11. The original name of Regina was:
    a) Buffalo Hill   **b)** No Man's Land
    c) Pile O'Bones   **d)** Granny's Town

12. The name Regina was decided upon because:
    a) it was the name of the first woman to settle there
    b) it was named for Queen Victoria
    c) the natives called it by that name
    d) it was meant to be Rejoin

13. Edmonton was named by William Tomlinson in honour of:
    a) King Edward   **b)** his son
    c) a section of London, England   **d)** his father

14. Iqaluit was first established as:
    a) James Bay   **b)** Artic Bay
    c) Baffin Island   **d)** Frobisher Bay

15. Yellowknife received its name from:
    a) the colour of the tools used by the natives   **b)** the gold that was found there
    c) the colour of the women's hair   **d)** the colour of the water

Answer Key

1. **a) Bytown**. It was named in honour of Colonel John By of the Royal Engineers, to whom the British government entrusted the construction of the Rideau Canal. It was named Ottawa in 1855.

2. **b) Trade**. It is derived from the Algonquin word "adawe" which means to trade.

3. **c) St. John the Baptist.** Newfoundland is believed to have been discovered on June 24, 1497, the feast of St. John the Baptist.

4. **b) George Monatgu Dunk.** He was the Earl of Halifax.

5. **b) Fredericktown.** It was named after His Royal Highness Frederick, Bishop of Osnaburg

6. **b) the wife of King George III.** Her name was Queen Charlotte.

7. **c) narrow river**. It is derived from the Amerindian word "Kebek" meaning strait or narrow river.

8. **b) Champlain**. The name was noted by Champlain in 1615.

9. **a) trees standing in water.** It is derived from a Mohawk word.

10. **b) dirty water.** The name is from the Cree "Winnipi" which can be translated as "dirty" or "murky" water.

11. **c) Pile O' Bones**. The name was changed to Regina in 1882.

12. **b) it was named for Queen Victoria.** The Governor General named it in honour of his wife's mother - Queen Victoria.

13. **c) a section of London, England.** He gave it this name in honour of the birthplace of John Peter Pruden, a clerk of the Hudson's Bay Company.

14. **d) Frobisher Bay.**

15. **a) the colour of the tools used by the natives.** Their tools were made from yellow copper.

Underground to Canada

The last stop on the **Underground Railroad** for slaves travelling by this route was freedom in Canada. The term "underground Railroad" was a fanciful name for a network of homes and people who helped escaping slaves reach their goal of being free. It stretched from the banks of the Ohio River through Vermont to Canada East. The slaves travelling on this above-ground network had to hide during the day and find their way through forests during the night. They were hidden in secret rooms and in sacks. The name originated from a slave-owner in pursuit of a runaway slave who lost his trail on the banks of the Ohio River. He shouted that the abolitionists must have a railroad under ground.

Major routes to freedom taken by runaway slaves

One of these slaves who escaped to Canada was Josiah Henson. He later became the hero of the famous novel, "Uncle Tom's Cabin", which Abraham Lincoln said was the cause of the Civil War in the United States. Harriet Tubman, also called Grandma Moses, travelled back and forth between Canada and the United States leading slaves to freedom.

The Underground Railroad played a very important part in Canada's past and especially in its relationship with the Confederacy during the American Civil War. Circle the correct answer to complete each of the following statements:

1. The houses and barns of those sympathetic to the slaves were called:
   a) stopovers   **b)** stations   **c)** refills   **d)** mug ups

2. The slaves used the _____ as a compass.
   a) North Star   **b)** moon   **c)** sun   **d)** Northern Lights

3. Josiah Henson spent _____ years as a free man in Canada.
   a) 25   **b)** 10   **c)** 40   **d)** 50

4. By 1830, there were estimated to be _____ former slaves living in Ontario.
   a) 500   **b)** 1000   **c)** 20,000   **d)** 50,000

5. Josiah Henson established a settlement of freed slaves in:
   a) St. Catharine's   b) Dresden
   c) Toronto   d) Peterborough

6. Anderson Ruffin Abbott was the first Black _____ in Canada.
   a) minister   b) politician
   c) doctor   d) police officer

7. William Hall was the first Canadian to be awarded:
   a) a university degree   b) the Victoria Cross
   c) a university scholarship   d) the 649 jackpot

8. Blacks who came to Canada as Loyalists received:
   a) the same as the Whites   b) more land than the Whites
   c) less land than the Whites d) land that was no good for farming

9. Many slaves came to Canada:
   a) as slaves   b) during the War of 1812
   c) looking for work   d) on their way to England

10. The escaped slaves who came to Nova Scotia were given:
    a) licences of occupation   b) no land at all
    c) well-paying jobs   d) a ticket on the next ship to Africa

11. It took the Blacks in Nova Scotia _____ years to gain ownership of their farms.
    a) 10   b) 6   c) 25   d) 2

12. Many of the escaped slaves who came to Canada before and during the Civil War:
    a) returned to the United States   b) settled in the West
    c) returned to Africa   d) settled in Ontario

13. Slavery did exist in Canada, particularly in:
    a) Ontario   b) Newfoundland   c) Quebec   d) Nova Scotia

14. Slavery was abolished in British North America in:
    a) 1793   b) 1812   c) 1834   d) 1843

15. Harriet Tubman made _____ trips between Canada and the United States to lead slaves to freedom.
    a) 22   b) 19   c) 25   d) 16

Answer Key

1. **b) stations.**

2. **a) North Star**

3. **d) 50** - He died at the age of 94, having lived the last 50 years as a free man.

4. **c) 20,000**

5. **b) Dresden.** He established a settlement at Dawn, near present-day Dresden, with other fugitive slaves.

6. **c) doctor** - His father was an escaped slave who came to Canada in 1835. He was a tobacconist who became wealthy and paid for his son's university education.

7. **b) the Victoria Cross.** William Hall was the Nova Scotian born son of an ex-slave. He received the Victoria Cross in 1857 during the mutiny of the British army in India.

8. **d) land that was no good for farming.** They did receive the promised amount of land, but the land that was given to them was mainly barren.

9. **b) during the War of 1812.** They were offered freedom by the British if they would enlist in the British military.

10. **a) licences of occupation.** This meant that they could live on the land, but they were never allowed to sell it. It was intended to protect them from landgrabbers.

11. **c) 25** - The freed slaves spent 25 years before they finally gained control of their own land and the licences of occupation were abolished.

12. **a) returned to the United States.** After Lincoln announced the Emancipation Proclamation in 1863, many of the slaves who had come to Canada returned to the United States.

13. **d) Nova Scotia.** Many of the Loyalists who came to Nova Scotia were slave owners and brought their slaves with them.

14. **c) 1834.** Slavery was abolished in all of British North America in 1834, but it had been outlawed in Canada East in 1793.

15. **b) 19**

Name: _____

World War I

When Britain entered the First World War on August 4, 1914, it was automatically assumed that Canada and Newfoundland would be involved in the war as part of the British Empire. Meetings were hastily called in Ottawa and St. John's to discuss what part they would take in this war. The first hastily equipped Canadian contingent set sail from Gaspe on October 3, 1914 and the next day the convoy was joined by volunteers from the Newfoundland Regiment.

War affected all aspects of life. At home, women became workers in the factories and when the war was over in 1918, they had won the right to vote. There were endless recruitment drives for soldiers. Many young Canadians and Newfoundlanders lost their lives on foreign soil and many returned home with English and Scottish brides.

Circle the letter of the correct answer to each of the following:

1. When the war broke out in August 1914, most Canadians believed it would be over:
   a) by Christmas
   b) within two years
   c) by summer
   d) almost immediately

2. Newfoundland was not part of the Canadian contingent because:
   a) they did not like the Canadians
   b) they wanted to fight on their own
   c) they were not part of Canada
   d) they were allies of the Germans

3. In the Battle of the Somme, _____ Canadians were killed.
   a) no
   b) 100
   c) 24,000
   d) 50,000

4. In the Battle of the Somme, 700 Newfoundland soldiers were killed. This number represented _____ % of the whole Newfoundland Regiment.
   a) 10
   b) 50
   c) 40
   d) 90

5. In Newfoundland, it was easier for _____ to go to war.
   a) politicians
   b) fishermen
   c) townspeople
   d) women

6. During the First World War, people living in Canada who had originally come from countries at war with Canada were:
   a) sent back to that country
   b) refused the right to vote
   c) forced to join the army
   d) forced to work in the factories

7. The War Measures Act allowed the government to:
   a) take away people's property   b) refuse to let people work
   c) force people to farm for a living d) force people to go fishing

8. The riots in the streets of Quebec were caused by:
   a) the newspaper reports   b) conscription
   c) the police   d) the cost of living

9. After the war was over, Canada owed:
   a) one million dollars   b) ten million dollars
   b) two billion dollars   d) twenty million dollars

10. After the war, Newfoundland owed:
    a) two billion dollars   b) fifteen million dollars
    c) ten million dollars   d) nothing

11. The First World War has been called:
    a) the Mother of all Wars   b) the Last War
    c) the Great War   d) the War to End all Wars

12. The Treaty of Versailles which ended the First World War also:
    a) created Denmark and Sweden
    b) created the British Commonwealth of Nations
    c) joined Canada and the United States
    d) joined France and England

13. Unrest in Canada after the war caused many:
    a) people to leave   b) people to come to Canada
    c) strikes and marches   d) more jobs to be created

14. After the war, Canada and Newfoundland:
    a) became separate countries   b) became one country
    c) became enemies   d) started their own war

15. The strikes of 1919 created:
    a) another war   b) a third political party
    c) a new language   d) different kinds of jobs

Answer Key

1. **a) by Christmas**.

2. **c) they were not part of Canada**. Newfoundland did not become part of Canada until 1949.

3. **c) 24,000** - Over a million men lost their lives in this battle.

4. **d) 90** - This was the largest loss of life suffered by Newfoundlanders in the war.

5. **c) townspeople** - It was easier for townspeople to go to war, because the livelihood of a whole village would be threatened if too many fishermen were gone during the fishing season.

6. **b) refused the right to vote.** They had to be Canadian citizens for fifteen years.

7. **a) take away people's property.** The War Measures Act gave the government wide ranging powers including the right to confiscate property, introduce censorship, and impose other controls on the people.

8. **b) conscription.** The French-Canadians were opposed to conscription because they thought it was aimed vindictively at them.

9. **c) two billion dollars.** The government had borrowed this money directly from the people at large as Victory loans.

10. **b) fifteen million dollars.** This amount was impossible to pay off.

11. **c) The Great War.**

12. **b) created the British Commonwealth of Nations.**

13. **c) strikes and marches.** There were few jobs and returning soldiers faced an inflation-ridden economy.

14. **a) became separate countries**. They were made full members in the League of Nations.

15. **b) a third political party.** The labour movement began to take an active part in politics.

World War II

When the Second World War broke out in 1939, Newfoundland was still a separate country from Canada. By now, Canada was a fully independent nation and was not automatically drawn into the war. Newfoundland, under the Commission of Government, was still in the same situation as it had been in 1914. Canada's entry into the war was almost as automatic as Newfoundland's because the majority of opinion in the country was on the side of the British.

For the first time, North American people feared air raid strikes and vessels were sunk in the St. Lawrence River. The government of Mackenzie King wanted to minimize the commitment of Canada to the war effort and there was no major recruitment drive to boost the army of 4000. Quebec still denounced Canada taking any part in the war. The French-Canadians still feared conscription of the First World War even though King promised that he would not use this method. As one country in Europe after another fell to the advancing German army, it seemed that Canada would have to prepare to defend itself on its own soil. Canada was the second most powerful country on Britain's side.

What do you know about the part played by Canada in the Second World War? Circle the letter of each correct answer.

1. The British Air Training Plan allowed _____ trainees to pass through bases in Canada.
   a) 100,000   **b)** 130,000   **c)** 140,000   **d)** 200,000

2. Under the N.R.M.A. Ottawa began to:
   a) take an inventory of its able-bodied men   **b)** pay people more money
   c) send European people back home   **d)** refuse entry to immigrants

3. The massive Mutual Aid program:
   a) paid people not to work   **b)** paid people higher salaries
   c) provided credit to allied countries   **d)** allowed more immigrants into Canada

4. American bases were established in:
   a) Ontario   **b)** British Columbia   **c)** Prince Edward Island   **d)** Newfoundland

5. Japanese people living in Canada were:
   a) sent to internment camps   **b)** forced to serve in the army
   c) sent back to Japan   **d)** sent to the United States

6. In 1944, the _____ began in Canada.
   a) war against Japan   b) The New Democratic Party
   c) family allowances   d) interest free loans

7. _____ began in Canada in 1940.
   a) Canada Pensions   b) Unemployment Insurance
   c) Student Loans   d) Welfare

8. Conscription was introduced in:
   a) 1940   b) 1941   c) 1944   d) 1946

9. The victorious Allies of the Second World War set up:
   a) the League of Nations   b) the Canadian Alliance
   c) the United Nations   d) The Social Credit Party

10. Mackenzie King thought Hitler:
    a) was a very strong man   b) was nothing to worry about
    c) would cause a lot of trouble d) might invade Canada

11. The King-Roosevelt Conference resulted in:
    a) Canada sending workers to the United States
    b) the two nations becoming enemies
    c) the two nations blending their economies
    d) the two nations agreeing not to fight Japan

12. During World War II, a German submarine was apprehended in:
    a) Ottawa, Ontario   b) Lunenburg, Nova Scotia
    c) Bay Bulls, Newfoundland   d) Montreal, Quebec

13. The largest influx of immigrants to Newfoundland and Canada after the war was from:
    a) the Jewish   b) the war brides   c) the Scottish   d) the Germans

14. NATO was created to:
    a) separate North America from the rest of the world
    b) punish the German people
    c) recruit people for the Armed Forces
    d) prevent the Soviet Union from causing another war.

15. Two major airports that were built in Newfoundland to transfer troops to Europe were:
    a) St. John's and North Sydney   d) Stephenville and Argentia
    c) Gander and Goose Bay   d) Mount Pearl and Corner Brook

Answer Key

1. **b) 130,000** - Ottawa haggled before taking on the commitment for 130,000 trainees to pass through bases in Canada.

2. **a) take an inventory of its able-bodied men**. Canada would have to respond to the need for more troops in Europe.

3. **c) provided credit to allied countries**. The government raised money for this effort by selling war bonds.

4. **d) Newfoundland**. Anxious to involve the United States in the war, the British took 50 out-dated American destroyers in return for 99-year leases on bases in Newfoundland.

5. **a) sent to internment camps**. The Canadian government recently apologized to the japanese Canadians for their treatment of them.

6. **c) family allowances**

7. **b) Unemployment Insurance** - These two programs were part of the government's plan for post-war recovery.

8. **c) 1944**. Only one contingent of conscripted troops went overseas before the war ended.

9. **c) the United Nations** - The victorious Allies set up a permanent peacetime organization called the United Nations.

10. **b) was nothing to worry about.** He described him as "an insignificant little peasant".

11. **c) the two nations blending their economies.** The war increased the production of central Canada and this put Canadians all across the country to work.

12. **c) Bay Bulls, Newfoundland**. During the war, Bay Bulls was an important base leased to the Canadians.

13. **b) the war brides**. Many soldiers returning home had married while overseas and brought their brides home with them.

14. **d) prevent the Soviet Union from causing another war.** Intensifying hostilities between the Communist and capitalist countries promoted Canada and other Western countries to form the North Atlantic Treaty Organization.

15. **c) Gander and Goose Bay.**

Two Solitudes

Canada has always been portrayed as a country without prejudice. However, this is not what the history of Canada tells us. In the 1890s Canada was a country warring within itself. Catholics hated Protestants, the West hated the East, and the Maritimes and Newfoundland hated central Canada. Management would not talk with labour, Conservatives would not dine with Liberals, and divorced persons were not accepted in society.

Business and social connections were formed within the confines of religion. Charitable organizations would aid only those of their own faith. Canadians in any one part of the country saw themselves as different from those in the other parts.

How much do you know about this period in Canadian history?

1. The Maritime Provinces had become so resentful of Confederation that it was difficult in Nova Scotia to get people to celebrate:
   a) Christmas   **b)** Easter   **c)** Dominion Day   **d)** Armistice Day

2. The people in Manitoba hated the people in central Canada because of:
   a) the hanging of Louis Riel   **b)** the American Civil War
   c) the R.C.M.P   **d)** the Canadian Pacific Railway

3. A major argument in Manitoba was the issue of:
   a) the Metis   **b)** the Manitoba Schools Question
   c) making Winnipeg the capital   **d)** the Red River Cart

4. In Quebec, an election was won by Honore Mercier who displayed the:
   a) Maple Leaf flag   **b)** the Union Jack
   c) the flag of France   **d)** the Stars and Stripes

5. Bishop Lafleche of Quebec wanted:
   a) Newfoundland to join Quebec   **b)** annex New England
   c) Quebec to join the United States   **d)** Quebecers to move to Nova Scotia

6. In 1896, the Catholics in Ottawa defeated a plan to build a public library because:
   a) they did not like to read   **b)** they had to pay taxes
   c) the Bishop could not censor the books   **d)** their children would have to read

7. The Canadian exhibit at the World's Fair in Chicago in 1893 was a disaster because:
   a) no one showed up to see it
   b) the two commissioners refused to speak to each other
   c) it arrived too late
   d) the Americans would not let it be seen

8. The choices for Prime Minister of Canada after the death of Sir John A. Macdonald were determined by:
   a) education   **b)** political aspirations
   c) religion   **d)** race

9.) The Protestant Protective Association took a solemn vow that they would not:
   a) hire Blacks   **b)** hire Catholics
   c) hire Chinese   **d)** hire women

10. Methodists and Presbyterians to Quebec to:
   a) convert the natives   **b)** convert the Anglicans
   c) convert the heathen Catholics   **d)** convert the politicians

11. John Abbott resigned as Prime Minister after only a year because:
   a) he was ill
   b) he did not like politics
   c) he did not like the antagonism between the religions
   d) he moved to China

12. The Northwest Territories abolished:
   a) drinking   **b)** the French language
   c) playing cards   **d)** dancing

13. Catholics were told it would be a mortal sin if they:
   a) voted for Laurier   **b)** went dancing
   c) moved to the Maritimes   **d)** moved to the United States

14. Laurier's policy of not getting involved was called the:
   a) easy way out   **b)** sunny way
   c) uninvolvement   **d)** misinterpretation

15. The prejudice which existed between French Catholics and English Anglicans in Quebec has been called Canada's:
   a) Civil War   **b)** Revolution
   c) Holy War   **d)** Rebellion

Answer Key

1. **c) Dominion Day.** This is now called Canada Day.

2. **a) the hanging of Louis Riel.** Louis Riel was seen as a hero to the Metis of Manitoba and Saskatchewan.

3. **b) the Manitoba Schools Question.** The French wanted to have separate schools where the French language and the Roman Catholic religion were taught.

4. **c) the flag of France.** He was in favour of Quebec separation.

5. **b) annex New England.** He said that too many Quebecers had moved to New England that it should be made part of Quebec.

6. **c) the Bishop could not censor the books.**

7. **b) the two commissioners refused to speak to each other.** One was Catholic and the other Protestant.

8. **c) religion.** The support the Prime Minister received depended on whether he was Catholic or Protestant.

9. **b) hire Catholics.**

10. **c) convert the heathen Catholics.**

11. **c) he did not like the antagonism between the Protestants and Catholics.**

12. **b) the French language.**

13. **a) voted for Laurier.** Wilfrid Laurier, the Prime Minister, refused to take sides in the debate over the Manitoba Schools Question.

14. **b) sunny way.** His policy was to leave things alone and let them work themselves out.

15. **c) Holy War.** It was not only a disagreement between French and English, it was also based on religion.

Name: _____

The Fathers of Confederation

The term **Fathers of Confederation** refers to the men who attended the conferences in Charlottetown, Quebec and London to plan and establish the Constitution upon which the Confederation of the British North American colonies into the country of Canada. The following people have been recognized as the Fathers of Confederation:

Sir John A. Macdonald	George Brown	Sir Frederic Carter
Sir Adams George Archibald	Sir Alexander Campbell	Edward Barron Chandler
Sir George Etienne Cartier	Jean-Charles Chapais	George Coles
James Cockburn	Robert Barry Dickey	Charles Fisher
Sir Alexander T. Galt	John Hamilton Gray	Lt. Col. John Hamilton Gray
Thomas Heath Haviland	William Alexander Henry	Sir William Pearce Howland
John Mercer Johnson	Sir Hector-Louis Langevin	Jonathan McCully
Andrew Archibald MacDonald	William McDougall	Thomas D'Arcy McGee
Peter Mitchell	Sir Oliver Mowat	Edward Palmer
William Henry Pope	John Willliam Ritchie	Sir Ambrose Shea
William Henry Steeves	Samuel Tilley	Charles Tupper
Etienne-Paschal Tache	Edward Whelan	Robert Duncan Wilmot

Which one of these Fathers of Confederation fits each of the following statements?

1. He would not allow the Intercolonial Railway to proceed until a widow had received compensation for a cow that had been killed by a train.

    _____

2. He was against Confederation and wanted things to remain as they were.

    _____

3. He wrote the **British North America Act**. _____

4. He duelled with Edward Palmer and challenged James C. Pope to a duel as well.

    _____

5. He was the chairman of the Charlottetown Conference. _____

6. He made recommendations to the British government regarding the lands question on Prince Edward Island. _____

7. He suggested the word **Dominion** for the name of the new country, Canada.

    _____

8. He wanted to place restrictions on who could be elected to the House of Assembly in Newfoundland. _____

9. He originally favoured Canada joining the United States. _____

10. He had the nickname of Wandering Willie. _____

11. He served as governor of the Bahamas. _____

12. He oversaw the completion of the Canadian Pacific Railway and the expansion of the Welland Canal. _____

13. He was an ally of Papineau in the Rebellions of 1837. _____

14. He made the most important handshake with John A. Macdonald in Canadian history. _____

15. He was nicknamed "My Little Nun" by John A. Macdonald. _____

16. He established the Canadian currency of dollars and cents. _____

17. He objected to the power of the Senate. _____

18. He was a great orator and delivered many speeches in favour of Confederation.

    _____

19. He was responsible for the power of the legislature to act in provincial affairs.

    _____

Name: _____

Prime Ministers Puzzle

```
C H R E T I E N T T E N N E B
A M N B V C X Z N A S D F U J
M A C K E N Z I E T S B P Y O
P A L D F N E D R O B H O T J
B E A G H L O N U M P T U R N
E W R R T O K O A I O U Y E M
L F K A S E I B L T I P T W A
L L E W O B N N T R U P T Q H
Z P N E D S G M S U Y E O R N
X Y E N O R L U M D T R B E E
T H O M P S O N P E R F B N H
Y B N O S R A E P A E D A R G
H Y E N O R E I R U A L S U I
D I E F E N B A K E R Q W T E
T R A B O B D L A N O D C A M
```

Word List:

Macdonald	Mackenzie	Abbott
Thompson	Bowell	Tupper
Laurier	Borden	Meighen
King	Bennett	St. Laurent
Diefenbaker	Pearson	Trudeau
Clark	Turner	Mulroney
Campbell	Chretien	

Answers

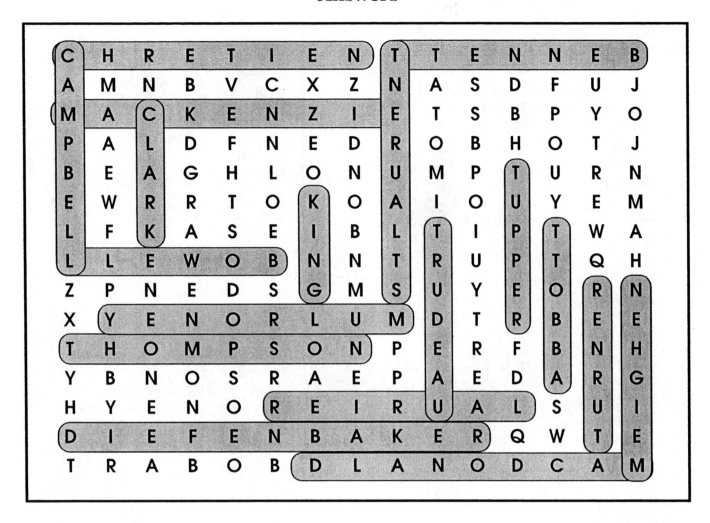

Name: _____

Canadian Outlaws

When one speaks of outlaws, the first names that come to mind are those of the outlaws of the American West. Canada has had its share of outlaws and pirates who posed problems for Canadian society. Some have left colourful stories in the history of Canada and its folklore and have inspired songwriters and storytellers. A few have become legends as heroes, but most of them led tragic and violent lives.

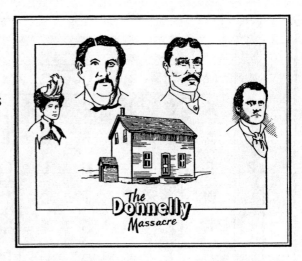

The Donnelly Massacre

How much do you know about Canada's outstanding villains?

1. Who was the murderer who was arrested by Canada's "Great Detective", John W. Murray?

    _____

2. Which bank robber was the son of a policeman? _____

3. Which gangster was known to his friends as "Old Creepy"?

    _____

4. Which pirate ransacked the small communities of Newfoundland?

    _____

5. Who was known as "The Canadian Jesse James"? _____

6. Which murderer was a doctor who used poison to kill his victims?

    _____

7. Who was known as "The Gentleman Bandit"? _____

8. Who was known as "The Megantic Outlaw"? _____

9. Who was the man who shot Thomas D'Arcy McGee? _____

10. What was the name of the Irish family who lived in Ontario and terrorized their neighbours?

    _____

Answer Key

1. **Reginald Birchell** conned two young men into paying him 500 pounds each for the purchase of a farm near Woodstock. He planned to kill the men and keep the money. He shot one of them and was arrested. He was hanged in Woodstock.

2. **Edwin Alonso Boyd** spent his youth as a hobo and served in the Canadian Armed Forces in the Second World War. He began robbing banks as a lone bandit. He was captured in 1951, but escaped to form the Boyd Gang. He was finally caught and eventually parolled from prison.

3. **Alvin Karpis** was a professional bank robber and kidnapper. He was a gunman for the Barker Gang during the Great Depression. He served 26 years in Alcatraz. In 1969, he was parolled and deported from the United States to Canada.

4. **Peter Easton**

5. **Norman Ryan** was a bank robber who was sentenced to life in prison. He was parolled and spoke out against crime. He was killed while robbing a liquor store.

6. **Thomas Neill Cream** was believed by some to be Jack the Ripper.

7. **Bill Miner** was one of the most infamous stagecoach robbers of the Old West.

8. **Donald Morrison** was the son of Scottish settlers who farmed near Lake Megantic. He is also known as "The Canadian Rob Roy".

9. **Patrick James Whelan** was convicted of shooting McGee and accused of being a member of the Fenians. He claimed to be innocent, but he was hanged anyway.

10. **The Black Donnellys** were an Irish family who held a feud with their neighbours for over twenty years. They were killed by a vigilante mob.

Name: _____

The Canadian Labour Movement

A large working class emerged in Canada in the nineteenth century with the increase of industrialization. Up until then, most Canadians had been self-employed, supporting themselves by farming, fishing or producing goods in small workshops. The family was the centre of the economy and every member played a part in the production of goods.

Industrialization changed the way work was organized. Work began to be completed in large factories using complex machinery. Work was repetitious and less rewarding even though it had become more efficient. Children worked in factories and were paid very little. They had to work to help their families. Early in the twentieth century, laws were passed preventing children from being employed in the factories and were put in school instead.

Women filled many jobs in the new factories and were employed as servants, housekeepers, secretaries, teachers and nurses. They had to fight their way into universities especially in medical and law faculties. They had fewer opportunities for advancement and were paid less than men.

Circle the letter of the correct response in each of these statements about the Canadian Labour Movement.

1. The first strike in Canada occurred in:
   a) 1910
   b) 1794
   c) 1856
   d) 1947

2. The first unions were often:
   a) illegal
   b) supported by government
   c) composed of women
   d) supported by the natives

3. The Trade Unions Act in 1872:
   a) outlawed unions
   b) would not allow women to work
   c) made unions legal
   d) forced families to work in factories

4. In 1872, working hours were:
   a) increased from ten to fourteen hours a day
   b) decreased from ten to eight hours a day
   c) decreased from fourteen to twelve hours a day
   d) decreased from twelve to nine hours a day.

5. One of the most successful unions in Canada in the 1880s was the:
   a) Canadian Auto Workers   b) Iron Workers
   c) Knights of Labour   d) Canadian Union of Public Employees

6. Labour Day was first celebrated in:
   a) 1881   b) 1872
   c) 1909   d) 1925

7. The first Canadian Department of Labour was created in:
   a) 1872   b) 1894
   c) 1909   d) 1900

8. The most dramatic strike in Canadian history was the:
   a) Loggers Strike   b) Winnipeg General Strike
   c) Postal Workers Strike   d) Auto Workers Strike

9. In the Winnipeg General Strike, _____ ended with the city under military patrol.
   a) Bloody Saturday   b) Bloody Sunday
   c) Bloody Monday   d) Bloody Tuesday

10. During the Great Depression, the federal government set up work camps where single men received wages of:
    a) $5.00 a day   b) 20 cents a day
    b) 50 cents a day   d) $2.00 a day

11. The Rand Formula required all workers:
    a) to wear uniforms   b) take specialized training
    c) take scheduled breaks   d) pay union fees

12. The first workers' candidate was elected to Parliament in:
    a) 1960   b) 1872
    c) 1867   d) 1939

13. The New Democratic party evolved from the:
    a) Cooperative Commonwealth Federation   b) the Social Credit Party
    c) the Western Reform Party   d) the New Canadian Party

14. Today, women make up _____ of the work force.
    a) 65%   b) 35%
    c) 45%   d) 25%

Answer Key

1. **b) 1794.** A group of fur traders in Rainy River, Ontario went on strike for better wages.

2. **a) illegal.** Members often went to jail for being part of a union.

3. **c) made unions legal.**

4. **d) decreased from twelve to nine hours a day.** People marched in the streets of Ontario and Quebec in support of decreasing the hours of work.

5. **c) Knights of Labour.** This American union came to Canada in 1881 and had strong support in Quebec.

6. **b) 1872.** It was declared a national holiday in 1894.

7. **c) 1900.** William Lyon Mackenzie became the first Minister of Labour in 1909

8. **b) Winnipeg General Strike.** 30,000 people joined in this strike.

9. **a) Bloody Saturday** - In an effort to break the strike, police fired on the crowd, killing one man and wounding several others.

10. **b) 20 cents a day.** They also received room and board.

11. **d) to pay union fees.** Workers were required to pay union fees whether they belonged to a union or not.

12. **b) 1872.**

13. **a) Cooperative Commonwealth Party**.

14. **c) 45%** - The most dramatic shift in labour in Canada has been the increase in the amount of work women do outside the home.

The Canadian Constitution

The British North America Act of 1867 declared that Canada had a constitution similar to that of Great Britain. In the 1950s Canada's Constitution was made up of six components:

- The British North America Act
- The Acts of the British Parliament
- The Acts of the Canadian Parliament
- Court Decisions
- Customs and Traditions
- Other

In 1982, the Prime Minister, Pierre Trudeau, decided that Canada should have its own constitution which would be separate from that of Britain. Thus began a long process which was called **Bringing home the Constitution**.

How much do you know about this process and the Canadian Constitution?

1. "Bringing home the Constitution" has also been called:
   a) "legalizing the Constitution"   **b)** "Making Canada a separate country"
   c) "patriating the Constitution"   **d)** "Trudeaumania"

2. The Statute of Westminster (1931) recognized:
   a) Canada was in North America
   b) Canada had full independence in the British Commonwealth
   c) Canada was essentially British
   d) Canada was north of the United States

3. The rights of Canadian citizens are entrenched in the:
   a) British North America Act   **b)** Confederation Act
   c) Quebec Act   **d)** Canadian Charter of Rights and Freedoms

4. Which of the following is not mentioned in the Canadian Constitution?
   a) the Cabinet   **b)** the Prime Minister
   c) the provinces   **d)** the territories

5. The first attempt to 'bring home the Constitution' failed because:
   a) the British government would not allow it
   b) only the provinces wanted it
   c) all the provinces could not agree on a formula
   d) the Prime Minister would have more power

6. In 1980, the issue of changing the Constitution was an attempt to:
   a) make Canada independent   **b)** defeat Quebec separatism
   c) make the British look foolish   **d)** give more power to the Senate

7. The secret meeting which resulted in a compromise for amending the Constitution has been called the:
    a) Trudeau Compromise   **b)** Chretien Compromise
    c) Kitchen Compromise   **d)** Cuisine Compromise

8. The only province that did not agree to the amendment was:
    a) Ontario   **b)** Nova Scotia   **c)** Manitoba   **d)** Quebec

9. The amending formula that was agreed upon says that _____ of the provinces must agree to the changes.
    a) 100%   **b)** 67%   **c)** 50%   **d)** 90%

10. An attempt to bring Quebec into the Constitution was called the:
    a) Meech Lake Accord   **b)** Atlantic Accord
    c) Quebec Accord   **d)** Ontario Accord

11. The Charlottetown Accord attempted to:
    a) amend the Constitution
    b) make Nunavut a province
    c) bring Quebec into the Constitution
    d) make Cape Breton a separate province

12. The Meech Lake Accord guarantees that:
    a) Quebec can never leave Canada
    b) Ontario can never take over the North
    c) Cape Breton will never be a separate province
    d) Quebec has a distinct society

13. The Parallel Accord proposed by Frank McKenna dealt with:
    a) the rights of women
    b) the fishery
    c) the mining industry
    d) the residence of the Prime Minister

14. In order for a new province to be admitted to Canada, there must be:
    a) at least 100,000 people living there   **b)** unanimous approval
    b) at least four electoral districts   **d)** Senate approval

Answer Key

1. **c) "Patriating the Constitution".**

2. **b) Canada had full independence in the British Commonwealth** and that no law made in Britain would affect Canada.

3. **d) Canadian Charter of Rights and Freedoms.**

4. **a) the Cabinet.** It is one of the customs that has developed over the years.

5. **c) all the provinces could not agree on a formula.** They could not agree on an amending formula by which the Canadian Parliament would be able to change the Constitution.

6. **c) defeat Quebec separatism.**

7. **c) Kitchen Compromise.** It was actually developed in an informal meeting in a kitchen.

8. **d) Quebec.**

9. **b) 67%** - Any changes must be agreed to by two thirds of the provinces.

10. **a) Meech Lake Accord.**

11. **c) bring Quebec into the Constitution.** This was the second attempt to do so.

12. **d) Quebec has a distinct society.**

13. **a) the rights of women.** It also dealt with other unresolved issues.

14. **b) unanimous approval** by all the other provinces and territories.

Name: _____

Canadian Inventions

Solve the riddles to find out about these Canadian Inventions.

1. Half of the traditional bowling game, invented by T. E. Ryan of Toronto in 1909.

   _____

2. Helps to make riding in a train more comfortable, invented by Henry Ruttan in 1858.

   _____

3. Helps to trim the abdomen, invented by Dennis Colonello in 1984.

   _____

4. Helps to close your coat or pants, invented by Gideon Sundback in 1913.

   _____

5. Helps to send messages under the sea, invented by Frederick Newton Gisborne in 1857.

   _____

6. Helps you to talk to someone in another province, invented by Alexander Graham Bell in 1876.

   _____

7. Helps you to see something happening in a faraway land, invented by Reginald A. Fessenden in 1927.

   _____

8. Helps to clear your driveway of snow, invented by Arthur Sicard in 1925.

   _____

9. Helps to clean up oil spills, invented by Richard Sewell in 1970.

   _____

10. Helps you pass the time by playing an educational game, invented by University of Toronto students Chris Haney and Scott Abbott.

    _____

11. Helps you dig your spuds effortlessly, invented by Alexander Anderson in 1856.

    _____

12. Helps to stop the train, invented by George B. Dorey in 1913.

    _____

13. Helps you have mashed potatoes without the mess, invented by Edward A Asselbergs in 1962.

_____

14. An easy way to water your lawn, invented by the Real McCoy.

_____

15. Helps to apply paint evenly, invented by Norman Breakey of Toronto in 1940.

_____

16. Helps people with diabetes, invented by Banting, MacLeod , Best and Collip in 1922.

_____

17. Helps you wrap up your refuse, invented by Harry Wasylyk in 1950.

_____

18. A game played with a hoop and a ball, invented by James Naismith in 1891.

_____

19. A cooling drink with Canada in its name, invented by John A. McLaughlin in 1907.

_____

20. Help for the blind when using a computer, invented by Roland Galaneau in 1972.

_____

21. Help for ships when traveling in foggy weather, invented by Robert Foulis in 1859.

_____

22. An alternative to using whale oil in lamps, invented by Doctor Abraham Gesner in 1846.

_____

23. A baby's delight, invented by Olivia Poole in 1959.

_____

24. An early form of sonar, invented by Reginald A. Fessenden in 1919.

_____

25. Helps you to enjoy your photographs, invented by Wilson Markle in 1983.

_____

Name: _____

Research a Famous Canadian Inventor

Research a famous Canadian inventor and their invention. Write a paragraph about what made this inventor famous.

_____

_____

_____

_____

_____

_____

_____

_____

_____

_____

_____

_____

_____

_____

_____

_____

_____

_____

_____

_____

_____

_____

_____

_____

_____

Name: _____

Famous Women in Canadian History

Research a famous female Canadian and write an essay on some unknown facts of their life.

_____
_____
_____
_____
_____
_____
_____
_____
_____
_____
_____
_____
_____
_____
_____
_____
_____
_____
_____
_____
_____
_____
_____
_____
_____
_____
_____
_____
_____
_____

Answer Key

Pictographs: *(page 8)*

1. star   2. moon   3. sun   4. sunrise   5. noon   6. fish   7. water bird   8. moose or deer
9. canoe   10. war   11. young tree   12. old tree   13. Great Spirit   14. river, stream
15. rain, cloudy   16. come   17. see   18. speak   19. dream   20. mountains

Native Legend: *(page 9)*

1. leaves, slippers   2. stalks   3. necklaces   4. corn cakes   5. corn kernels
Eastern Corn Planters

The Franklin Expedition: *(page 47)*

Sir John Franklin's men ate food from tins that were made of lead. Some theories propose that the men died from lead poisoning. The survivors died as they tried to walk south.

Gold Rush Puzzle: *(page 58)*

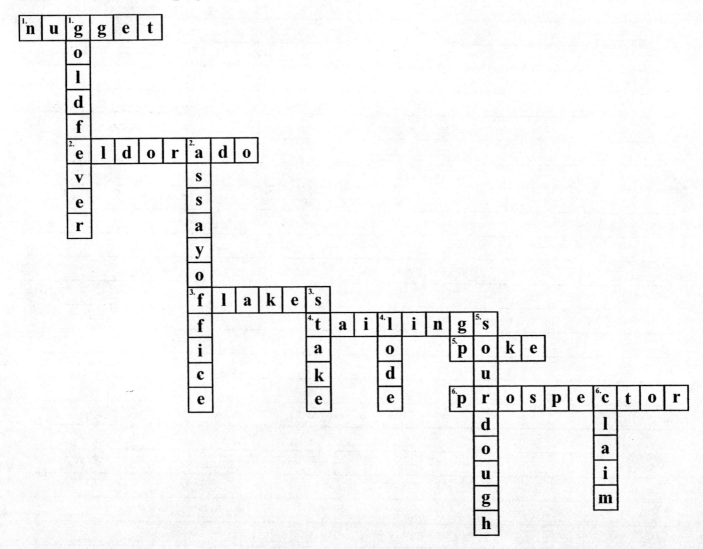

The Alaska Boundary Dispute: *(page 59)*

The British were far more concerned with their relations with the United States than the actual settling of the boundary dispute. Canada also had a weak case for their arguments.

Fathers of Confederation: *(page 78-79)*

1. Peter Mitchell
2. Edward Palmer
3. John A. Macdonald
4. George Coles
5. Lt. Col. John Hamilton Gray
6. William Henry Pope
7. Samuel Leonard Tilley
8. Frederic Carter
9. Alexander T. Galt
10. William McDougall
11. Ambrose Shea
12. Charles Tupper
13. Georges Etienne Cartier
14. George Brown
15. Jean-Charles Chapais
16. Alexander T. Galt
17. William Henry
18. Thomas D'Arcy McGee
19. Oliver Mowat

Canadian Inventions: *(page 90-91)*

1. 5 pin bowling
2. air conditioned coach
3. abdomenizer
4. zipper
5. undersea telegraph cable
6. telephone
7. television
8. snowblower
9. slicklicker
10. Trivial Pursuit
11. potato digger
12. railway car brake
13. instant mashed potatoes
14. lawn sprinkler
15. paint roller
16. insulin
17. garbage bags
18. basketball
19. Canada Dry ginger ale
20. computerized Braille
21. automatic fog horn
22. kerosene
23. Jolly Jumper
24. fathomete
25. colour film

Bibliography

Schemenauer, Emma. <u>Native Canadians: Today and Long Ago</u>, Nelson Canada, 1985

<u>The Junior Encyclopedia of Canada</u>

Stanford, Frances. <u>The Prime Ministers of Canada</u>, The Solski Group, 2002

Stanford, Frances. <u>The Fathers of Confederation,</u> The Solski Group, 2002

Stanford, Frances. <u>The Development of Western Canada</u>, The Solski Group, 2001

Stanford. Frances. <u>Canada's Confederation</u>, The Solski Group, 2002

Howard, Richard , Sonia Riddoch and Peter Watson. <u>Canada Since Confederation</u>, Copp Clark Pitman, 1976

Carroll, Joy. <u>Pioneer Days</u>, Natural Science of Canada, 1979

Greenwood, Barbara. <u>Gold Rush Fever</u>, Kids Can Press, 2001

Schemenauer, Emma. <u>John A. Macdonald</u>, Grolier Ltd., 1987

Moore, Christopher. <u>Samuel de Champlain </u>, Grolier Ltd., 1985

Corkum, Nadja. <u>How Canada Got Its Capital</u>, The National Capital Commission, 1975

Hayes, John. <u>The Nation Builders</u>, Copp Clark, 1968

Lunn, Janet. <u>The Story of Canada</u>, Lester Publishing, 1992

Collins, Robert. <u>The Age of Innocence</u>, Natural Science of Canada, 1977

Stephenson, William. <u>Dawn of the Nation</u>, Natural Science of Canada, 1977

Publication Listing

Publication Listing

Code #	Title and Grade	Code #	Title and Grade	Code #	Title and Grade	Code #	Title and Grade
SSN1-27	Unicorns in Literature Gr. 3-5						
SSJ1-44	Upper & Lower Canada Gr. 7-8						
SSN1-192	Using Novels Canadian North Gr. 7-8						
SSC1-14	Valentines Day Gr. 5-8						
SSPC-45	Vegetables B/W Pictures						
SSY1-01	Very Hungry Caterpillar NS 30/Pkg Gr. 1-3						
SSF1-13	Victorian Era Gr. 7-8						
SSC1-35	Victorian Christmas Gr. 5-8						
SSF1-17	Viking Age Gr. 4-6						
SSN1-206	War with Grandpa SN Gr. 4-6						
SSB1-91	Water Gr. 2-4						
SSN1-166	Watership Down NS Gr. 7-8						
SSH1-16	Ways We Travel Gr. P-K						
SSN1-101	Wayside Sch. Little Stranger NS Gr. 4-6						
SSN1-76	Wayside Sch. is Falling Down NS 4-6						
SSB1-60	Weather Gr. 4-6						
SSN1-17	Wee Folk in Literature Gr. 3-5						
SSPC-08	Weeds B/W Pictures						
SSQ1-04	Welcome Back – Big Book Pkg 1-3						
SSB1-73	Whale Preservation Gr. 5-8						
SSH1-08	What is a Community? Gr. 2-4						
SSH1-01	What is a Family? Gr. 2-3						
SSH1-09	What is a School? Gr. 1-2						
SSJ1-32	What is Canada? Gr. P-K						
SSN1-79	What is RAD? Read & Discover 2-4						
SSB1-62	What is the Weather Today? Gr. 2-4						
SSN1-194	What's a Daring Detective NS 4-6						
SSH1-10	What's My Number Gr. P-K						
SSR1-02	What's the Scoop on Words Gr. 4-6						
SSN1-73	Where the Red Fern Grows NS Gr. 7-8						
SSN1-87	Where the Wild Things Are NS Gr. 1-3						
SSN1-187	Whipping Boy NS Gr. 4-6						
SSN1-226	Who is Frances Rain? NS Gr. 4-6						
SSN1-74	Who's Got Gertie & How...? NS Gr. 4-6						
SSN1-131	Why did the Underwear ... NS 4-6						
SSC1-28	Why Wear a Poppy? Gr. 2-3						
SSJ1-11	Wild Animals of Canada Gr. 2-3						
SSPC-07	Wild Flowers B/W Pictures						
SSB1-18	Winter Birds Gr. 2-3						
SSZ1-03	Winter Olympics Gr. 4-6						
SSM1-04	Winter Wonderland Gr. 1						
SSC1-01	Witches Gr. 3-4						
SSN1-213	Wolf Island NS Gr. 1-3						
SSE1-09	Wolfgang Amadeus Mozart 6-9						
SSB1-23	Wolves Gr. 3-5						
SSC1-20	Wonders of Easter Gr. 2						
SSY1-15	Word Families Gr. 1-3						
SSR1-59	Word Families 2,3 Letter Words Gr. 1-3						
SSR1-60	Word Families 3, 4 Letter Words Gr. 1-3						
SSR1-61	Word Families 2, 3, 4 Letter Words Big Book Gr. 1-3						
SSB1-35	World of Horses Gr. 4-6						
SSB1-13	World of Pets Gr. 2-3						
SSF1-26	World War II Gr. 7-8						
SSN1-221	Wrinkle in Time NS Gr. 7-8						
SSPC-02	Zoo Animals B/W Pictures						
SSB1-08	Zoo Animals Gr. 1-2						
SSB1-09	Zoo Celebration Gr. 3-4						